BLOOMSBURY
CURRICULUM BASICS

Teaching Primary Art and Design

BLOOMSBURY CURRICULUM BASICS

Teaching Primary Art and Design

By Emily Gopaul

BLOOMSBURY

LONDON · OXFORD · NEW YORK · NEW DELHI · SYDNEY

Bloomsbury Education
An imprint of Bloomsbury Publishing Plc
50 Bedford Square, London, WC1B 3DP, UK
29 Earlsfort Terrace, Dublin 2, Ireland

www.bloomsbury.com

BLOOMSBURY and the Diana logo are trademarks of Bloomsbury Publishing Plc

First published in Great Britain 2017

A catalogue record for this book is available from the British Library.

ISBN
PB: 978-1-4729-4593-8
ePub: 978-1-4729-4591-4
ePDF: 978-1-4729-4594-5

6 8 10 9 7

Typeset by Newgen Knowledge Works Pvt Ltd., Chennai, India
Printed and bound in India by Replika Press Pvt. Ltd.

To find out more about our authors and books visit www.bloomsbury.com. Here you will find extracts, author interviews, details of forthcoming events and the option to sign up for our newsletters.

For the talented young artists at Millbank Academy and busy teachers, old and new.

Online resources accompany this book at: www.bloomsbury.com/BCB-Teaching-Art.

Please type the URL into your web browser and follow the instructions to access the resources. If you experience any problems, please contact Bloomsbury at: companionwebsite@bloomsbury.com

Other titles in the Bloomsbury Curriculum Basics series:

Teaching Primary History by Matthew Howorth

Teaching Primary Science by Peter Riley

Teaching Primary French by Amanda Barton and Angela McLachlan

Teaching Primary Spanish by Amanda Barton and Angela McLachlan

Teaching Primary Computing by Martin Burrett

Teaching Primary Geography by Stephen Scoffham and Paula Owens

Teaching Primary PE by Jazz Rose

Contents

Introduction

What the National Curriculum for England says

The National Curriculum changed in 2014, and the revised curriculum is a succinct document that prompts minimal changes regarding its *Purpose of study* and *Aims*. It is likely that those schools with an already good practice of teaching art and design, and those that remain informed by the 1999 Qualifications and Curriculum Authority schemes of work are still comfortably meeting the government requirements. That said, the lack of detail around *Subject content* could offer an opportunity for change as well as posing some challenges. The National Curriculum (2014) does not offer any guidance about content, it certainly does not dictate what should be taught; there are no explicit details about which processes, genres, artists or styles of art to teach – it tells us the aims of the art and design curriculum but without the specifics about how to achieve them. There is an intentional emphasis on allowing schools the freedom to create their art and design curriculum content.

There are no statuary requirements on time allocated to the teaching of art and design, and this could be viewed as a strength, allowing schools to review their timetables and adopt an achievable goal for regular art and design lessons. Schools can adapt their art and design curriculum to fit timetable restrictions whilst also ensuring a comprehensive coverage of the subject across the key stages. As it is not compulsory for schools to teach the traditional half-termly schemes of work, teachers are free to respond to the needs of the children, without the impetus to stretch projects out until the end of the term, or indeed to leave work unfinished because the new term has begun. Teachers and schools should use this freedom to revisit, review and extend the children's learning in art and design as necessary.

Books like this one are here to offer expertise to those wishing to redesign or revamp their art provision and to lend guidance to new and experienced teachers alike.

For more information about how the author, Emily Gopaul, can support you with art in your school, visit www.theprimaryartclass.com.

The 2014 National Curriculum for art and design: Key Stages 1 and 2

Purpose of study

Art, craft and design embody some of the highest forms of human creativity. A high-quality art and design education should engage, inspire and challenge pupils, equipping them with the knowledge and skills to experiment, invent and create their own works of art, craft and design. As pupils progress, they should be able to think critically and develop a more rigorous understanding of art and design. They should also know how art and design both reflect and shape our history, and contribute to the culture, creativity and wealth of our nation.

Aims

The national curriculum for art and design aims to ensure that all pupils:
- produce creative work, exploring their ideas and recording their experiences
- become proficient in drawing, painting, sculpture and other art, craft and design techniques
- evaluate and analyse creative works using the language of art, craft and design
- know about great artists, craft makers and designers, and understand the historical and cultural development of their art forms.

Attainment targets

By the end of each key stage, pupils are expected to know, apply and understand the matters, skills and processes specified in the relevant programme of study.

Key Stage 1 (KS1)

Pupils should be taught:
- to use a range of materials creatively to design and make products
- to use drawing, painting and sculpture to develop and share their ideas, experiences and imagination
- to develop a wide range of art and design techniques in using colour, pattern, texture, line, shape, form and space
- about the work of a range of artists, craft makers and designers, describing the differences and similarities between different practices and disciplines, and making links to their own work.

Key Stage 2 (KS2)

Pupils should be taught to develop their techniques, including their control and their use of materials, with creativity, experimentation and an increasing awareness of different kinds of art, craft and design.

Pupils should be taught:
- to create sketchbooks to record their observations and use them to review and revisit ideas
- to improve their mastery of art and design techniques, including drawing, painting and sculpture with a range of materials [for example, pencil, charcoal, paint, clay]
- about great artists, architects and designers in history.

The following table shows a breakdown of the National Curriculum requirements for each key stage in bold. Below each National Curriculum requirement is a description of how the lessons within this book meet and extend them.

KS1 pupils should be taught:	KS2 pupils should be taught:
to use a range of materials creatively Children use a range of art and non-art materials such as pencils, charcoal, crayons, poster paint, watercolour paint, food colouring, mud, sticks, modelling clay, etc. They have time to explore the potential of the materials as well as creating pieces of art with them. **to design and make products** Children work towards practical outcomes contained within one lesson or spread across a few. Outcomes are designed and made by the children.	**to develop their techniques** KS2 schemes of work build on the foundational learning that took place in KS1. Children use more advanced techniques and build on prior learning as they move through the key stages. **to develop their control and their use of materials** Children learn how to use specific techniques and materials to achieve the desired outcome – they make with purpose. They do this through a combination of taught skills and individual exploration of the potential of materials. **to use techniques and materials with creativity, experimentation and an increasing awareness of different kinds of art, craft and design.** Children are encouraged to exploit the potential of materials, finding appropriate ways to express their ideas, experiences and imagination. Schemes of work provide a broad example of traditional and contemporary art.
to use drawing, painting and sculpture to develop their ideas, experiences and imagination KS1 schemes encompass all three areas plus collage and printing. Schemes include opportunities for children to use their ideas, experiences and imagination as starting points and stimuli throughout. **to use drawing, painting and sculpture to _share_ their ideas, experiences and imagination** Final pieces in KS1 encompass all three areas plus collage and printing.	**to create sketchbooks to record their observations and use them to review and revisit ideas** Most schemes include a preparatory phase of generating ideas, design and collecting visual information – this can be completed in sketchbooks if they are available. As the children work on their final outcomes, they should be encouraged to test techniques and materials, jot down additional ideas and develop concepts and compositions in their sketchbooks. Where sketchbooks are not practical, a folder or handmade sketchbook will suffice. More about this in the **Storage of work** section (page 13).
to develop a wide range of art and design techniques using colour, pattern, texture, line, shape, form and space The formal elements of art are built into all schemes of work and, where appropriate, taught discreetly.	**to improve their mastery of art and design techniques, including drawing, painting and sculpture with a range of materials [for example, pencil, charcoal, paint, clay]** Schemes of work support the acquisition of specific skills and techniques in drawing, painting and sculpture, in addition to collage and printing. Children are also encouraged to use materials independently, selecting the appropriate materials and techniques to develop their concepts. Children continue to refer to the formal elements as they master techniques in a variety of materials. Students experience selecting materials that they believe to be appropriate to realise their ideas.

about the work of a range of artists, craft makers and designers	about great artists, architects and designers in history
Children are introduced to a range of artists who work in a variety of media. They discuss and respond to the key artworks.	Schemes of work and lessons link to a range of key artworks, in a variety of disciplines, and the children participate in discussions inspired by them.
how to describe the differences and similarities between different practices and disciplines Schemes of work and lessons link to a range of key artworks, in a variety of disciplines, and the children participate in discussions and practical work inspired by them.	The children use their knowledge and experience of the formal elements to engage in analysis of key artworks. Children are familiar with the historical and geographical context of the key artworks, and they should be encouraged to map them out chronologically on a timeline. As mentioned in the ***Classroom display*** section (page 12).
how to make links between different practices and disciplines and their work The children produce their practical work in response to these key artworks; making links through the concept, material, technique or subject.	

Fig. 1A: Table showing how the lessons within this book meet and extend the National Curriculum requirements for each key stage.

Within the domain of art and design there is such a broad and eclectic world of artists, architects, craftspeople and designers and although the National curriculum does not require it, teachers should feel free to supplement the lessons in this book. It can be valuable to seek out inspiration and organise visits from local people working in these fields and it will also be beneficial to your art and design curriculum to make links with and plan visits to galleries and museums. Extra art lessons can be added to generate work inspired by topics in the other subject areas, and extra-curricular craft clubs could offer a chance to work with some of the materials and skills not covered in the lessons here (e.g. textiles, clay or wire), although art and design should also have status as a discrete subject.

Why art and design matters

Whether you are a trainee teacher, newly qualified teacher or experienced teacher, you may have noticed the widespread pressure in primary schools to regularly teach and gain results in literacy and numeracy. Thankfully, the teaching of art and design is rarely subject to such pressure, but a consequence of this is that the frequency, status and quality of art and design lessons differs vastly between schools. Although most schools endeavour to achieve a broad and balanced curriculum, the reality is that time constraints and data driven approaches can result in subjects like art and design being side-lined. Unlike other subjects, and due to the lack of government specifics about art and design, decisions about how art and design is taught are sometimes low priority. Whether art and design subject content in your school is decided by individual class teacher, an art co-ordinator, senior leadership or a mixture, it is vital that primary-aged children are regularly exposed to art, artists and creativity and that art and design is as valued as other subjects.

We live in a visual world and as human beings we are constantly interpreting images and inferring meaning from our visual environment. We live in a world that is rich in cultural histories – arts and crafts are ripe for us to access and understand, via the Internet, films, books, galleries and museums. We have growing contemporary art and design industries and, increasingly, organisations of all sorts recognise the potential of creative thinkers to grow businesses. Learning skills and techniques in art and design gives children an additional language, a visual one, that provides another means by which to express ideas and process their thoughts.

The term STEM has long been recognised in education, and many schools recognise an additional drive to integrate the areas of science, technology, engineering and maths in a way that promotes student-led inquiry. Lately this has shifted to include art, i.e. STEAM; esteemed organisations such as The Big Draw (www.thebigdraw.org/the-big-draw) promote the addition of art to the model, and recognise the economic, social and spiritual value of the arts. The TED talk 'Do Schools Kill Creativity' by Sir Ken Robinson is widely watched and quoted. In it he 'champions a radical rethink of our school systems, to cultivate creativity and acknowledge multiple types of intelligence'; it is well worth a watch.

Art and design lessons provide opportunities for children to work in ways that differ from the other subject areas, in ways that support the development of well-rounded children. A quality art and design curriculum should:

- Provide opportunities for children to share and discuss their subjective opinions about their own work and the work of others in ways that are respectful.
- Allow children time to create with opportunities to problem solve and review and refine their work.
- Teach children skills and processes with a range of materials.
- Have progression mapped across key stages.
- Offer chances for children to explore the potential of different materials, making independent discoveries.
- Place art and design in a wider context, making it relatable for the children by making links to current affairs and popular culture.
- Give children access to knowledge and information about art and artists.
- Introduce children to a range of male and female artists from different times and places.
- Support children in making links between art and design and their learning in other subject areas.
- Allow children to use their own ideas and experiences to create work that is valued.
- Provide an environment where children feel safe taking risks and are not intimidated by 'getting it wrong'.
- Allow chances for children to work alone and collaborate.
- Inform children about creative industries and careers that exist.
- Empower children to pursue creative endeavours, should they wish to do so.

From the point of view of the primary school teacher, when you teach art and design, you see a different aspect to the children in your care. During an art lesson it is easy to see that this subject appeals to an important and innate part of children's nature, one that should be nurtured in well-rounded individuals. You may be responsible for children who, despite challenges in other subject areas, are able to gain a sense of achievement and pride during art lessons. Children you teach may go on to have successful careers in the field, if they are inspired and encouraged to do so, or perhaps they will come to rely on art as an outlet vital to maintaining a healthy and happy lifestyle.

How this book works

The book is divided into three sections: KS1, Lower KS2 and Upper KS2. Each key stage has between eight and ten schemes of work, and each scheme of work has three lesson plans – the lessons can be extended or reduced to best fit the requirements of the class and time.

All schemes of work cover skills in one or more of the five main areas of drawing, painting, collage, sculpting and printing, and some combine skills or allow the children to select their materials. The lessons are designed to support learning about one or more of the formal elements of art. Works of art called 'key artwork(s)' are embedded into almost every lesson, and they provide the stimulus for discussions as well as a point of inspiration for the practical part of the lessons. The lessons are planned so that the children can make visual *and* verbal links between their art and the key artwork(s). The key artworks range from prehistoric cave paintings to more contemporary pieces, by well-known and lesser-known artists. You will find more information about the five main skill areas, formal elements and key artwork(s) on pages 10–11.

Each topic begins with:

- **In 30 seconds...** – a brief overview of the topic.
- **Key artwork(s)** – the artwork used as stimulus for discussion and practical work.
- **What do I need to know?** – information about the key artwork(s), artist and genre.
- **Vocabulary and Useful links** – definitions of key terms and suggestions for useful websites related to the lessons; where possible a link is provided for the key artwork(s). For a list of general art terms, see the **Glossary** (page 182).

Within each of the three lessons for each scheme of work, you will find clear direction regarding what you will need in terms of materials and resources, as well as any practical preparations that you need to make before teaching the lesson. The plans include a section on **Getting started** which will advise you on how to begin each lesson; usually this involves discussing the key artwork and explaining how it links to the practical part of the lesson. The analysis of the key artwork can always be extended or developed into written tasks, it can also be slotted into any shorter time slots available in the day and then referred to in the practical lesson later. There are clear lists of class activities and plenaries. The third and final lesson plan includes recommendations for how to extend learning through additional lessons or suggestions of adaptations that can be made to the lessons provided. You will also find any relevant cross-curricular suggestions at the end of each scheme of work. Assessment is not included in great detail but it is assumed that the teacher will build self, peer and teacher assessment throughout; there are suggestions for this in the **Assessment** section (pages 14–16).

The schemes of work are somewhat sequential in that the skills and techniques being taught build upon the prior learning as set out in previous schemes within the book. That said, it would be possible to adapt any lesson in the book to meet the needs of your children, although it might prove useful to teach the children some basics on the applicable skill area and formal element first. It is recommended that KS2 teachers periodically revisit the schemes set out for KS1, either for their information or as a recap lesson with the children. For example, there is a scheme of work in the Lower Key Stage 2 section, *Fernand Léger: Drawing and painting* (page 68), which is predominantly a painting scheme. Before embarking upon this KS2 scheme, the teacher could provide opportunities for the children to briefly revisit the tasks in the KS1 scheme *Colours and painting* (page 32).

The five main skill areas

The lessons in this book cover five main skill areas; some lessons combine two or more of these main skill areas. Please see also the section on the National Curriculum (page 2).

Drawing

We know that drawing is considered one of the earliest forms of human communication, discovered in caves in Asia and Europe dating up to 40,000 years old. It is perhaps lesser known that prior to the Renaissance period, drawing was mainly used as a preparatory exercise for producing paintings or sculptures, and was not necessarily considered an art form.

From a teaching standpoint, drawing lessons are among the most easily executed art lessons as they can be quickly set up using a wide range of easily obtained materials. If you find yourself unable to teach any other art lessons for whatever reason, providing the children with opportunities to draw for different purposes (from imagination, memory, to design something or from observation) is highly recommended.

Drawing underpins many of the schemes of work in this book, as frequently it is how visual artworks, no matter what the final material or process, begin. In fact, it is how the design process takes place in many industries outside of the arts and it is a useful tool for children to possess to make their ideas and thoughts visible to others.

For the teacher keen to pinpoint attainment in art, information is more widely available about the developmental stages of drawing compared to the other skill areas. In brief, in the early years children will mainly draw to enjoy the sensation of movements involved with the process, and the incidental marks that appear because of this. Eventually, mark making leads children to discover how combinations of lines and shapes can communicate their ideas in a way that is understood by others. This realisation moves them towards a desire to record what they see, think and remember with some level of precision – sometimes leading to feelings of frustration when this is not straightforwardly attained.

The drawing lessons provided here for KS1 are focused on expressive mark making and making ideas visible, as well as some lessons about recording observations using line, tone, texture and shape. It is helpful to make a distinction with the children between drawing from imagination, memory and observation, although there may be times when the children are combining one or more of these.

Observational drawing

In upper and lower KS2, the drawing activities provided include some observational drawing lessons such as still life and portrait drawing. Periodic observational drawing tasks such as of an object or a person are useful to record progress, e.g. a simple self-portrait task could provide a tangible yearly assessment in art if your school requires it.

Observational drawing promotes careful consideration and concentration and encourages the children to notice details and review and refine their work as it develops – all important life skills. The drawing lessons for KS2 also include some specific technical skills, such as how to produce three-dimensional drawings and how to create a sense of perspective; these techniques provide children with instantly effective results and give them a real sense of accomplishment.

It is a fallacy that the teacher needs to be a talented artist to teach drawing lessons; a lack of drawing experience should not stop you from teaching drawing. In any case, it can be more effective to model to the children how we can *observe* details and look more carefully at the subject, rather than modelling the actual drawing yourself.

'Drawing is the primal means of symbolic communication, which predates writing and functions as a tool of conceptualization parallel with language.' (Deanna Petherbridge)

Painting

Painting is an area that can meet resistance with primary teachers because of the mess factor, but painting lessons needn't leave your classroom tables and floors looking like a Jackson Pollock work. It is entirely possible to 'train' children of all ages to clear tables and wash painting equipment if you make this part and parcel of the lesson itself – looking after the materials is just as vital as the actual painting activity, and it should be taught with the same level of commitment as any other lesson. That said, in KS1 it is advisable to have painting lessons at the end of the day or before lunchtime; younger children will love helping to tidy up but it is always better to have a bit of time to check over their handiwork.

The KS1 painting lessons in this book suggest the use of poster paints, which are the paints that are most readily available in primary schools. In fact, small sets of watercolour tins and shorter thin brushes work very well with younger children too and are infinitely easier to set up and pack away. Painting lessons in KS1 should involve the explicit teaching of how to handle the materials, i.e. how to load the brush with paint, how to wash the brush and how to paint neatly – great for fine motor skills, as well as extending the children beyond pure mark making with the brush. The KS1 lessons ensure that the children learn about primary and secondary colours as well as warm and cool colour groups.

The lessons provided ensure that by the end of KS2, the children are familiar with the complementary colours and can mix shades and tints of colours. They will experience using colour in a painting to express a mood that they wish to convey to the viewer. They will use a range of brush sizes and techniques for different effects and be able to confidently select their brushes for a specific purpose.

Painting exercises have the potential to link well to all of the formal elements and the lessons provided here try to exploit that, but for KS1, there is a particular affinity between colour and painting lessons. There are many paintings suggested as key artworks in the book and they range in style and approach, with the aim of exposing the children to a broad cross-section of art.

'Painting is concerned with all the 10 attributes of sight; which are: darkness and light, solidity and colour, form and position, distance and propinquity, motion and rest.' (Leonardo da Vinci)

Collage

The word 'collage' comes from the Old French verb 'coller', which means to stick or glue. Children enjoy the experience of cutting, ripping, arranging and glueing parts of different materials to create a complete image.

Collage lessons, similarly to painting, can be off-putting for class teachers due to the likelihood of ending up with a classroom carpet littered with bits of paper and small hands covered in glue. As with all the skill areas, it is imperative to teach 'care of the materials' and 'tidying away', as a vital part of the art lesson. Collage materials can be easily and cheaply sourced and can be as simple as old magazines and newspapers – if you have space, it is advisable to stock up on such items over time, so that you don't find yourself surreptitiously grabbing thirty copies of a free newspaper on the morning of a collage lesson. You could build a collection of materials with different textures and even group them in containers according to colours, like you would find in a paint palette. The children will enjoy collecting their own materials and delivering them into the collage boxes.

Although there is only one collage scheme of work provided here for KS1, collage tasks are especially good for developing fine motor skills and teaching the basics of cutting and glueing. For younger children, make a point of teaching them how to hold and use the scissors properly, moving the paper rather than their bodies as they snip not chop. It is in KS1 collage lessons that children can learn how to apply glue with sticks or spatulas, only dabbing glue onto the edges rather than smothering whole pieces of paper.

The KS2 lessons provided include photomontage and mosaic, both of which are considered types of collage.

'Popular culture isn't a freeze-frame; it is images zapping by in rapid-fire succession, which is why collage is such an effective way of representing contemporary life.' (James Rosenquist)

Printing

It is an almost primal impulse that a child, when presented with a tray of paint, is likely to place his or her hand inside it and proceed to make repeat prints on whatever surface is available. Likewise, a child's delight at seeing their footprint imprinted in a pile of mud or snow is somewhat inbuilt; some children's shoes even cater for this with specially designed soles. Although we might think of early art as being limited to cave paintings and drawings, the duplication of images by use of stamps into wet clay goes back to early Mesopotamian civilisation.

Printing lessons can be daunting or seem to require lots of specialist art equipment usually associated with the secondary art classroom. The lessons in the book for KS1 and KS2 however, suggest the use of easily acquired materials that aren't too specialist to use: collograph printing in KS1 and a form of lino printing using foam tiles in KS2. Both these techniques still provide good results and will offer a good, basic understanding of the printing process that can be built on when the children move up to secondary school.

Setting up the classroom for printing can require some extra time and effort. It is useful to think of the room in terms of printing stations with children working in pairs or small groups, rather than having each child printing at the same time. As the children will likely be producing multiple prints, you will need extra drying space, either a rack, hanging or if possible leave the work on tables to dry.

'The act of printing has always seemed to me a miracle, just such a miracle as the growing up of a tiny seed of grain to an ear – an everyday miracle, even the greater because it happens every day. One drawing is sown on the stone or the etching plate, and a harvest is reaped from it.' (Vincent van Gogh)

Sculpting

Through constructing, manipulating, carving and modelling, sculpture projects can be broad and use traditional or non-traditional materials – generally the outcome being a three-dimensional form of any scale. A distinction can be made between sculpture, which is usually made with the intention that the work will be viewed from any angle, and 'relief'. A piece of work in relief is generally made to be viewed from the front only, with a design that projects outwards from the surface.

When teaching sculpture to children, it is not always necessary to have them sketch or meticulously plan sculptures via drawing first. Often it is only through first-hand experience of using the materials that children can make informed design choices. It is often beneficial to get them using the materials straightaway in order to explore the potential of the materials at hand and independently problem-solve and discover techniques.

The sculpture lessons included in this book encourage the use of a range of materials and the production of work in different scales. If possible, try to block out more time than usual for sculpture lessons, as sculptures can be tricky to store and cumbersome to keep bringing out week after week. Larger sculpture work may also require you to rearrange the tables and chairs in the classroom – encourage the children to work standing for larger projects and always to view their sculpture work from all angles as they make it. A sculpture day or afternoon is a good idea, and the children will thank you for it.

'Painting is so poetic, while sculpture is more logical and scientific and makes you worry about gravity.' (Damien Hirst)

The formal elements of art

Pattern/Colour/Texture/Tone/Shape/Line
The formal elements of art can be described as the ingredients that make an artwork. How these elements are arranged, whether consciously or not, impacts the way that art is regarded and discussed. As such, an awareness of the formal elements is useful when discussing art *and* making art. The teaching of the formal elements as discrete lessons is more appropriate in KS1, and there are KS1 lessons included in this book on colour mixing and exploring types of line. As the children get older and more familiar with the formal elements, they should become an integral part of art and design lessons and discussions. With the basics having been taught early on, the children will begin to demonstrate a natural awareness of them when they make and analyse art. As a teacher leading discussions about art, the formal elements can provide a straightforward lens through which to initially view artwork and stimulate conversation. You could, for example, begin discussions with a focus on the types of colours that an artist has selected and speculate as to why he or she has chosen them, what mood they convey and how the work would change if a different palette of colours was used. It is important to remember that the formal elements can provide a way for the children to view not only paintings and art, but also their environment, and the language that they learn can help them to interpret the visual world at large.

For more information on the formal elements of art, see:
www.bbc.co.uk/schools/gcsebitesize/art/practicalities/elementsofart1.shtml

The key artwork(s)

A key artwork (or artworks) accompanies most of the KS1 lessons and all of the KS2 lessons provided. Although there are many other possible starting points for children's art lessons, these key artworks provide opportunities for the children to learn about art, the art world at large and artists. As well as this, the artworks often provide significant links to history and geography, and it is beneficial for the children to be able to make cross-curricular links in their learning. Through looking at and discussing the key artworks, the children infer meaning from images, and they increase their vocabulary – you should always insist on full sentence answers that utilise specialist vocabulary. By linking the children's practical work to a key artwork, embedding the formal elements and providing opportunities for the use of a range of materials, the children make progress in all the skill areas as well as gaining cultural enrichment.

The key artworks have been carefully selected to offer a broad range of influences, including artists old and new, male and female, from different backgrounds and specialisms. Each artwork has been selected to offer an insight into a material, technique, concept or genre and if all lessons are taught, the children will leave Year 6 with a well-rounded art education.

Information about the artist, title, material and date made is given in the **Key artwork(s)** section and links are provided to online versions of the artwork(s) in the **Useful links** section where possible. However, a simple Internet search of the key artwork and artist will provide you with a suitable copy of the image to use in a slideshow or worksheets – ensure that the images you source are of a high resolution. There are opportunities for discussion about the key artwork(s) built into the plans provided. It is recommended that you dedicate some time to the analysis of the artworks, and rather than simply supplying the children with information about the art or artists, you could scaffold questions to challenge the children to infer meaning for themselves. Looking at and responding to the artwork does not need to happen as part of an hour-long lesson; in fact, it can be a good task to do when you find your class with a spare ten minutes in the day. The work that the children do on responding to the key artwork will inevitably feed into their practical lesson when it comes around. Likewise, it is possible to lengthen the analysis part of the lessons to include more in-depth discussions and even some written exercises. For more ideas about discussing artworks see **Bloomsbury Online Resource IA**.

Through the lessons provided in the book, the children will notice and discuss aspects of the key artworks and then replicate them in their own work. This is not to say that the children are merely copying famous artworks – the point of stimulus is not limited to the materials or subject matter – sometimes the children are working with the same concept as the artist but with a totally different material, or the technique might be the same but the idea being developed is the child's own. The children will see how their art can share commonalities with famous art and they will be able to use specific vocabulary to discuss the key artworks and their work. The children will become confident art critics, able to share their opinions about art and make informed observations that will improve their own practical work.

Classroom organisation and general preparation

It is advisable to prepare for the lessons provided in this book by reading all three of the lesson plans in advance and making your own exemplary practical piece prior to teaching. This will enable you to understand the process that the children will experience and it will place you in good stead to pre-empt challenges and give pointers. It will also give you a practical idea about the materials that you will need for each lesson and how best to lay them out.

It is valuable to do some background reading about the key artwork(s) so that you feel confident leading discussions about it/them and answering any questions the children may have. Some essential information related to the key artwork(s) is provided and although you may not wish to share all of it with the children, it is helpful to know it. For further information, the relevant Wikipedia page is often useful and gallery websites can provide additional resources. Where relevant, extra weblinks have been included to help too. There are suggestions for general weblinks in the **Useful links** section at the end of the book.

In terms of setting up materials and equipment, over time it is possible to train the children to help you but you might find that this takes too much time out of their lessons. Art lessons scheduled at the start of the day or after break time allow you some freedom to set up, but failing that, it can be helpful to prepare materials in large trays, ready to be laid out on tables.

Demonstration area

It works well to have a designated demonstration area in your classroom, for showing the children the practical parts of the lesson and for gathering the children with their work for plenaries and assessment. This area could be a table or surface that you can regularly go to. Train the children to gather there sensibly – taller children at the back, no leaning on the table, etc. The lesson plans provided often direct you to conduct a demonstration or to ask the children to gather and look at their work; after a few practices the children should gather at the demonstration area quickly and efficiently as a natural part of any art lesson.

Slideshows

Most teachers regularly use slideshows to aid teaching and this is also a useful way to begin art lessons – with a sense of context and purpose. Before teaching any of the lessons, source a high-resolution version of the relevant key artwork(s) and place it or them into a slideshow, ready to view and discuss with the children. High-resolution images mean that you can zoom into the image to show details and focus discussions on particular areas of the work. It is advisable to test out how the image looks when you zoom in to it, before the lesson. Many of the images will be available on gallery websites with a built-in option to zoom in.

It is good practice to display the artwork how it might be exhibited in a gallery setting, i.e. with the title of the art, the artist's name, materials used and the date; it is useful for the children to get accustomed to using this basic information when viewing art. In some cases, the lessons provided direct you to gradually disclose information, such as the artist's name, to promote the use of clues to interpret the image. You may also want to include slides that introduce some of the key words alongside imagery related to them.

Another technique for encouraging the children to have in-depth discussions about the artworks is to reveal interesting or even obscure sections of the image for discussion, before unveiling the whole image. Most interactive whiteboards have this capability, but it is also possible to use *Microsoft Paint*™ or similar programs to crop segments of the image and then paste them into your slideshow.

Classroom display

Not all schools will have a dedicated art room and classroom display space can be limited; information for art lessons can be placed on portable boards and brought out for lessons, most school suppliers stock cardboard folding boards for table top displays which are useful for this. Space permitting, have a permanent display in your classroom of the information used regularly including the basics of colour, line, shape, tone, texture and pattern. If this is not possible, placemats or laminated handouts can be useful, when mixing colours, for example it could be helpful to have the colour 'recipes' on a placemat for the children to look at.

It is advisable to display a large world map in your classroom so that you can challenge the children to locate countries as they come up in lessons, e.g. where artists hail from or the scene of a painting. Easy access to the map will also facilitate you making cross-curricular links with geography and history.

Have a timeline either as a physical display or as a slide on a presentation, so that you can plot thumbnails of the key artworks that the children learn about chronologically. You could combine this display with significant dates in history and science.

Have keywords on display and refer to them when discussing the key artwork and the children's artwork, making links between the two. You could build this collection of words up with the children, as the discussions about the key artwork develop over lessons. You could even include art vocabulary in spelling tests.

Sentence starters can be helpful to support the children as they talk about art. Have a selection of these on display during every art lesson, e.g. *In this painting, I can see…* or *I think that this artwork has…*

Having displays of the children's artwork is a wonderful celebration, but it can also be beneficial to display work in progress, with a heading that says as much. Hang work on clothes pegs or tack it to walls around the room as it is being created. Don't be put off by the belief that displays should be of perfectly finished work. It is helpful to the artists to see their work as it develops and this will inform them as they refine their work in the next lesson.

Storage of work

The National Curriculum states that children in KS2 should 'create sketchbooks to record their observations' and 'use sketchbooks to review and revisit ideas'. This guidance need not mean the acquisition of expensive sketchbooks, the children could easily make their own with folded paper and the use of a stapler. If your budget does stretch to it, then sketchbooks are a great way of raising the profile of art and the children will love feeling like 'real' artists. Many of the preparatory stages of the lessons here require paper but the work could just as easily be made in sketchbooks.

A3 plastic folders or a large piece of paper folded in half can serve as good, affordable storage for children's artwork. You may want to allow children to take work home after each scheme, but it can also be useful to keep it all until the end of the year, or even throughout their time at school – this is a good way of tracking progression through a portfolio of work, for more information, see the **Assessment** section (pages 14–16). Portfolios also mean that you can hold exhibitions with a small collection of work from each child; these are great events for parents and staff to enjoy and they showcase the learning that is taking place in your art lessons.

You will need to have a space for drying work; a designated drying rack is useful but failing that, a clothes line with clothes pegs can work just as well. A good tip is to schedule art lessons at the end of the day or before lunchtime so that work can dry on tables overnight.

Materials order list

What follows is a list of materials required to teach the lessons in the book. Materials can be shared across year groups or key stages if teachers co-ordinate the schemes that they will be teaching.

- A1 or bigger newsprint paper
- A1 sheets of paper or rolls of paper to cover tables
- A1 white/beige paper
- A3 and A4 cartridge paper
- A3 coloured paper/card
- A4 card
- A4 envelopes or paper clips for storing loose paper/cuttings
- A4 photocopy paper
- Acrylic paints (optional)
- Air-dry clay
- Aprons
- Black fine liners
- Black pens
- Blu-Tack™
- Camera
- Chalks
- Charcoal
- Class set of faux flowers
- Clay tools
- Cling film
- Clipboards
- Colour wheel
- Colouring pencils
- Cotton buds
- Crayons
- Drawing pencils
- Erasers
- Fake gold leaf (from craft suppliers)
- Felt tips
- Fixative for chalk and charcoal or hairspray
- Flat headed brushes in various sizes
- Foam or polystyrene tiles for printing
- Glue sticks
- Gold glitter
- Gold pens
- Magazines
- Magnifying glasses
- Masking tape
- Mirrors (try to source mirrors that stand up or have some props to stand the mirror against)
- Modelling clay (Giotto is a good brand)
- Non-spill water pots (depending on seating, one between two is usually sufficient)
- Paint palettes
- Plastic shapes (borrowed from maths resources)
- Poster paints (at least primary and secondary colours)
- Printing ink
- PVA glue and glue spreaders
- Rollers for printing
- Scissors
- Scrap card
- Scrap paper
- Sketchbooks or A3 folders for storing work
- Small whiteboard and markers (one each)
- Synthetic brushes in various sizes, including size 2, 4 and 6
- Thick card/board
- Tissues for dabbing brushes
- Tracing paper
- Watercolour paint sets (depending on seating, one between two is usually sufficient)
- Watercolour paper (not used frequently)
- Wooden mannequins, enough for each child to see one.

Assessment

Assessment in art differs from other subject areas but is nonetheless valuable. It is sometimes difficult to ascertain which part of an art lesson requires assessment – after all, opinions on art are subjective! In art and design, it is far less useful for the children to 'mark' their finished artwork at the end of a project than it is to provide ongoing feedback throughout a project. Formative assessment, whether it be self, teacher or peer, is invaluable. The children will need time to review and refine their work as they go, they will also benefit from having you and their peers provide advice, tips and reminders about how to use the tools and techniques.

In terms of final pieces, although it is nice for children to take their work home, allowing children to keep a folder or portfolio throughout their time at primary school is a powerful form of assessment (photographs of work and children working can form the basis of this if their actual artwork is not available). The schemes of work in this book cover mainly painting, drawing, printing, collage and sculpting so it is possible to track progress in these areas over time.

It is the role of the teacher to watch how the children are using the tools and materials in the art lesson and address misconceptions; it will be obvious when a child needs support or verbal prompts to improve their technique. For example, if you see that a child who is supposed to be making an observational drawing has not glanced at the subject in a long time, then you know that he or she is not observing it well enough.

Through the discussions about the key artworks, you will be able to establish the children's understanding of how the formal elements are arranged to create a composition. It will also become evident how much the children know about the key artwork, and in KS2 you could formalise this with written assessments about the key artwork.

This book does not give many specific directions about when and how to use assessment, although it is assumed that you will endeavour to build teacher, peer and self-assessment into the lessons. What follows are suggestions that should be straightforward to integrate into your lessons and could become part and parcel of every art lesson.

Obviously, these suggestions do not consider the specifics of your school's marking policy, but if you can, I would argue that art lessons, like PE and music, should be subject to a different approach. Do not feel put off by needing to evidence your regular formative feedback; you know your students, and you know that this assessment has taken place and you and the important thing is that the child has been able to improve their work and develop a deeper understanding of the materials and processes.

As with all assessment, it is only fair to assess the children on what you have taught them, so being clear about your expectations is always a good place to start.

	KS1 Children should be able to:	KS2 Children should be able to:	Evidence
Responding to the key artwork	• Talk about the key artwork using specific vocabulary and referring to the formal elements, e.g. 'I can see different lines in the self-portrait.' • Share subjective views about the work, e.g. 'I like it because…' 'It reminds me of…' • Explain how their artwork is like the key artwork.	• Talk or write about the key artwork using specific vocabulary and referring to the formal elements. • Share subjective views about the work, e.g. 'I like it because…' 'It reminds of…' 'It makes me feel…' • Explain how their artwork makes connections to the key artwork.	**KS1** Video the children talking about their work. The teacher jots down comments on sticky notes and places them on the children's corresponding work. **KS2** Video the children reviewing their work. Children jot down comments on sticky notes and place them on their corresponding work. Children write an analysis of the work or answer teacher-set questions about it. Children write a newspaper article about the work.
The making process	• Use the materials and techniques in the way specified by teacher. • Improve their work by using equipment and techniques in a specialised way. • Verbally describe the materials they are using and share tips for using them safely and carefully. • Work on a sustained piece of art, reviewing and refining it over time.	• Use the materials and techniques in the way specified by teacher. • Improve their work by using equipment and techniques in a specialised way. • Verbally describe the materials, tools and processes and share tips with peers. • Work on a sustained piece of art, independently reviewing and refining it over time.	Photographs of the children working, e.g. close-up of hands doing the making/using the tools. Sticky notes written by teacher, transcribing what the children say.
The final piece	• Organise the formal elements • Use the materials and techniques to achieve the desired outcome, making visual links to the key artwork. • Talk about the final piece, describing the materials and tools used and how the work is like the key artwork.	• Demonstrate deliberate organisation of the formal elements/the use of the materials and techniques to achieve the desired outcome, making visual links to the key artwork. • Talk about the final piece, describing the ideas, processes, materials and tools used and how the work is like the key artwork. • Independently select appropriate tools and materials for the task.	The final piece in their portfolio. Discussions with the child. Child-written assessment of work with tick list of goals.

Fig. 1B: Ideas for assessment in art and design

Part 1
Key Stage 1

What does the KS1 curriculum say?

Pupils should be taught:

- to use a range of materials creatively to design and make products
- to use drawing, painting and sculpture to develop and share their ideas, experiences and imagination
- to develop a wide range of art and design techniques in using colour, pattern, texture, line, shape, form and space
- about the work of a range of artists, craft makers and designers, describing the differences and similarities between different practices and disciplines, and making links to their own work.

Curriculum content

KS1 art and design lessons should be distinctively different from KS2 lessons; lessons in Year 1 will probably be the children's first experience of art taught as a discrete subject and EYFS to Year 1 is a significant transition with big changes for the children. It is important that the lessons for KS1 meet the children where they are as well as extending their learning and laying the foundations of understanding and experience for future lessons.

It can be challenging to pitch KS1 lessons; teachers often want to facilitate creativity while also introducing an element of structure and progression. We want younger children to continue to exploit the potential of art as a tool for their personal imaginative expression, free from the expectation of producing a 'final piece'. However, it is also a good time for children to begin to experience the benefits of having a clear objective and a sustained piece of work that they return to for continued development. The lessons reflect both approaches and provide opportunities for explorative lessons *and* more structured, teacher-led lessons.

The KS1 lessons offer experiences that are divided into the skill areas of: drawing, painting, collage, sculpting and printing and the children have opportunities to use relevant materials, processes, techniques and vocabulary. The children will explore and discover first-hand the potential of media and techniques, whilst subtly developing control of a range of art tools and materials. The children should receive praise for proper use of the materials, tools and techniques but this should happen in a way that does not hold the children to account so rigidly as to stop any creative exploration. As the children are working, it is helpful to bring their attention to outcomes that they produce by verbalising the effect and showing them, e.g. 'Look at the way when you rolled the clay it made a sphere shape', or 'Can you show me again how you made that green colour?'.

The lessons here introduce children to the properties of some of the formal elements of art, covering line, shape, tone, texture and colour and these will be revisited throughout KS2. KS1 children should begin to express the links between their work and the key artworks, both visually and verbally, and children should feel confident sharing their instinctive opinions and feelings about their own art and the work of others. The lessons here support the children as they start to form an idea about how art began, what art is and what the role of the artist is. The lessons are a mixture of expressive and more structured exercises that will lay the foundations for further learning in KS2.

1 Drawing

Basics of drawing

In 30 seconds...

The lessons that follow are intended to give KS1 children a pacy and fun introduction to drawing with different tools and to achieve different effects. The three lessons will help the children to form an understanding of the elements that can make a drawing. They will begin observing the world in shapes, lines and tones and start to see the relationship between these elements. The children will begin to use drawing to translate the three-dimensional world into a two-dimensional drawing and use drawing to communicate an idea. The first lesson asks the children to listen to different genres of music and to respond by making marks on their paper. In the second lesson, the children will explore ways of using simple shapes and lines to create images of animals and the final lesson introduces tone through self-portraits.

Key artworks

Vincent van Gogh, *Fishing Boats at Saintes-Maries-de-la-Mer*, reed pen and ink, 1888 (see Figure 1A)
Pablo Picasso, *Le Hibou (The Owl)*, *Le Chameau (The Camel)* and *Le Chien (The dog)*, prints on paper, date unknown
Vincent van Gogh, *Self-portrait*, pencil and ink on paper, from 1887

What do I need to know?

The key artworks introduce the children to two of the greats: Vincent van Gogh and Pablo Picasso, and it could be a good chance to discuss questions such as, 'What is an artist?' and 'What do artists do?'.

Vincent van Gogh's *Fishing Boats at Saintes-Maries-de-la-Mer* drawing is one of a few studies and paintings that the artist made whilst taking a seaside trip to recover from a bout of poor health. Van Gogh was very skilled at drawing, and he believed that an artist should master drawing before all else; he prepared for many of his paintings with preliminary sketches. Much of the painting styles and brush marks that we associate with Van Gogh are evident in the lines of his drawings. This drawing was made with a reed pen and ink – the pen was made from local grass and the ink would once have been black but has since faded to a dull brown colour. This artwork provides an excellent example of how an artist can use different marks or lines to delineate areas and communicate visual information. Not only do the types of marks vary, but also the weight. This would have been challenging to achieve with a reed pen as opposed to a pencil. The artist has used a cascade of wavy lines to depict the rough waters at the forefront of the drawing and these cleverly recede into smaller dashes as the sea reaches the background. The reflections of the boats in the distance are shown by the absence of any lines. Although the man in the boat is made up of just a few lines, we can see that he is a fisherman and therefore assume that the boats are fishing boats which usually set sail early in the morning. The choppiness of the water and the blowing sails could suggest that it is a windy morning. The sky is made up of dots, and clouds are implied with the use of lighter marks.

Picasso was an animal lover and his dachshund dog, Lump, features in many of his works as well as other animals that the artist came across and enjoyed. The animals are depicted using minimalist lines and shapes but the drawings nonetheless capture the essence of the creatures and they are all instantly recognisable. These simple drawings by Picasso provide an excellent example of line and shape drawing for children and make it possible to see how three-dimensional shapes can be recorded with great effect in two-dimensional drawings. Picasso famously produced a series of eleven bull studies in around 1945, which begin with an academic and realistic drawing and show how the artist gradually simplified and abstracted the image, ending up with a simple line drawing much like the key artworks here. Although the bull series is a powerful example of abstraction and simplification, the key artworks chosen here are a more suitable for this age group.

It is estimated that Van Gogh made thirty-six self-portraits in ten years, perhaps fewer only than Rembrandt. The Van Gogh self-portrait is another example of the artist's use of line; this time it is possible to see how the artist has placed lines according to the contours of the face and its features. Unlike the previous drawing by Van Gogh, this one includes some cross-hatching and it is clear to see how the artist has used varying pressure on the pencil to achieve different tones – the eyes are as dark and intense as the artist's gaze.

- An **artist** is someone who makes art and Vincent van Gogh and Picasso are both very famous artists.
- Many artists like to **draw** and Vincent van Gogh used different types of **lines** such as dashes and wavy lines in his drawings.
- Some of Van Gogh's lines are thick and some are thin; some are light and some are dark.
- Picasso also made drawings and he liked to draw animals using simple lines and **shapes**.
- Van Gogh also drew a self-portrait in which he used lines, **tones** and **cross-hatching**.

Vocabulary

Artist: A person who creates art.
Cross-hatching: Shading with lines that cross over.
Draw: To produce a picture or diagram using lines and marks.
Line: A long mark or stroke.
Shape: The form or outline of an object.
Tone: The lightness or darkness of something.

Useful links

www.vangoghmuseum.nl/en/collection/d0432V1962r A clear image of Vincent van Gogh's self-portrait
www.wikiwand.com/en/Saintes-Maries_(Van_Gogh_series) Vincent van Gogh, *Fishing Boats at Saintes-Maries-de-la-Mer*

www.artyfactory.com/art_appreciation/animals_in_art/pablo_picasso.htm Picasso's bull series – not appropriate to show the children but demonstrates how Picasso simplified the bull drawing
www.artrepublic.com/articles/281-the-line-drawings-of-pablo-picasso-html Picasso animal drawings
www.slideshare.net/RodriguezArt/element-of-art-line-14756539 Online slideshow about line

Lesson 1 Expressive mark making with dots and lines

Key artwork
Vincent van Gogh, *Fishing Boats at Saintes-Maries-de-la-Mer*, reed pen and ink, 1888 (see Figure 1A)

You will need
- Crayons in a variety of colours
- Large pieces of paper (A1 works well) in white or beige folded or divided into six parts
- Access to YouTube or an MP3 player with speakers

Preparation
You will need to spend some time selecting five music tracks from different genres, e.g. classical, jazz, heavy metal, salsa. The idea is that each track evokes a very different mood. It is usually easier if you fold the paper before the lesson as young children may find this difficult. It is useful to have the crayons in a central tray or container so the children can select them easily as they respond to the music.

Getting started
Show the children the key artwork and explain that it is a drawing by Vincent van Gogh who was a great artist, discuss what an artist is. Begin by encouraging the children to describe what they can see in the drawing, bringing the discussion towards the fact that the drawing is made up of lines. Ask the children to think about why Van Gogh used those types of lines to show water. Look for answers that refer to the fact that Vincent van Gogh represented the movement of the water. Ensure that the children are aware of how the lines vary in direction, weight and thickness. Explain to the children that artists like to use different types of lines and marks in their drawings and that the lines and marks can show different things. Explain that the children will be trying to draw different types of lines and marks. Ask some children to name different types of lines and then draw them on the board for the class to see (examples include spirals or wavy lines). Tell the children that they are going to hear different types of music, and they will try to create different lines and marks to go along with each song. Tell them that the music might make them feel happy, calm, sad, etc. and so their lines and marks will probably change for each song. You could use one of the tracks to show how you might spend a few minutes listening to the music first and then use the crayon to fill one of the boxes on the paper with lines.

Class activities
- Play the first track, remind the children to silently listen and then use one of the boxes on their paper to fill with lines that come from listening to the music.
- Continue to play each track for two or three minutes each or read the room to see when most

children have finished drawing. It is helpful to leave a few minutes of silence in-between tracks to 'reset' the room.

- You might need to remind the children that they should be making lines – some might be tempted to scribble for each track.
- You could ask some of the children to share how the tracks make them feel after listening to each one.
- Remind the children that they can vary the type of line they use as well as the direction and thickness.

Plenary

Gather the children to look at their work and lead a discussion about the different lines and marks. Encourage the children to describe the types of lines and marks that they see in each other's work. Support them in using descriptive words, such as wavy lines, zigzag lines, straight lines, etc. You could encourage the children to make links between how the tracks made them feel and the types of lines they used, for example if heavy metal music made you feel angry, you might use big, dark zigzag lines. Look again at the key artwork and highlight that they have been artists just like Van Gogh, using lines and marks in their work. Ask the children to look around the classroom and identify different types of lines in their immediate environment.

Lesson 2 Shape and line animals

Key artworks

Pablo Picasso, *Le Hibou (The Owl), Le Chameau (The Camel)* and *Le Chien (The dog)*, prints on paper, dates unknown

You will need

- Whiteboards and pens, one each
- A3 cartridge paper folded into four sections

Preparation

Ensure that the whiteboard pens work and that children can easily access their boards. It is helpful to fold the paper for the children as they may find that difficult.

Getting started

Remind the children how good they were at using different lines and marks last lesson to show how the music made them feel, and recap the points about why artists use different lines and marks in their work. Explain that artists also use shapes and lines to make drawings of people or animals, and that using lines and shapes can make drawing things a bit easier. Show the children Picasso's drawings and lead a discussion about how, even though the artist has used simple lines and shapes, it is still possible to tell what he was drawing. Ask the children whether the animals by Picasso look how the actual animals look and explain that they are a meant to represent the animal not be a realistic drawing. Highlight the fact that Picasso loved animals (especially his dog, Lump), and he was very skilled at making drawings of three-dimensional animals using lines and shapes. Explain that the children will be working like Picasso, using simple lines and shapes to make drawings of animals. Ask the children to recap all the shapes that they know and make quick drawings of them on their whiteboards.

Class activities
- Explain to the children that you would like them to help you to use simple lines and shapes to draw a cat on your board. Ask children to share suggestions for the shapes that you use, e.g. a circle for the body, a smaller circle for the head, two triangles for the ears, one triangle for the nose, etc.
- Allow the children time to use their whiteboards and pens to draw a cat using lines and shapes; they could copy your example or use their own ideas.
- Give the children the challenge of drawing another animal such as a dog or a sheep. They should use shapes and lines only on their whiteboards.
- Ask the children to think of their own animal to draw on their whiteboards and then they can take turns to guess which animal the person next to them drew.
- Now the children have practised on whiteboards, allow them to draw four line and shape animals using the whiteboard pen on their paper. You could give them a list of four animals, e.g. a fish, a panda bear, a mouse and an elephant, or let them choose. It is fine if they practise each one on the whiteboard first.

Plenary
Gather the children to look at their work. Highlight the fact that all their drawings are made up of lines, marks and shapes, just like 'real' artists such as Picasso and Van Gogh. Ask the children to give each other feedback on their work and try to work out which animals their classmates have drawn. Ask the children to suggest what they would add to the drawings if they wanted to make them look more realistic, e.g. fur, patterns or colour.

Lesson 3 Self-portraits with tone

Key artwork
Vincent van Gogh, *Self-portrait*, pencil and ink on paper, from 1887

You will need
- Pencils
- A4 paper
- Mirrors – try to source freestanding mirrors or have some props ready to stand the mirrors up against

Preparation
Set the mirrors up so that each child can see themselves clearly.

Make an Internet search for a simple guideline to drawing the proportions of the face (see www.artyfactory.com/portraits/pencil-portraits/proportions-of-a-head.html). This information is useful for you to know and disseminate during the lesson.

Getting started

Ask the children to recap the different materials they have used to draw with and remind them how in previous lessons they have used lines, marks and shapes to make drawings. Recap the names of the artists, explaining that Vincent Van Gogh and Pablo Picasso are two of the most brilliant artists that lived. Tell the children that they are going to see another drawing by Van Gogh now and that it is known as a self-portrait because it is a drawing that he made of himself. Show the children the self-portrait and spend some time 'reading' the image and discussing how the artist might have been feeling judging by his expression, i.e. he looks serious because of his eyes and maybe a bit sad because of the way his mouth is set. Discuss with the children how they think Van Gogh would have known what he looked like – would he have used his imagination or memory? Tell the children that Van Gogh had to use a mirror to copy his face, so he had to draw and look at the same time. Tell the children that they will be using a pencil and a mirror to make their self-portrait, just like Van Gogh did. Bring attention to the way that some lines are darker than others and ask the children if they know how the artist did that. Demonstrate to the children how they can apply more pressure to a pencil to get a darker tone and less pressure to achieve a lighter tone. Show the children how some of the lines cross over each other and explain that this is known as 'cross-hatching'.

Class activities

- Give the children A4 paper, pencils and a mirror.
- Ask the children to look at themselves in the mirror and notice where their eyes are, i.e. they are not at the top of their head but halfway down.
- Ask the children to begin with the outline of their face – encourage them to fill the page and then draw their eyes halfway down. They should look in the mirror to add as many details of their eyes as possible. Use prior line and shape knowledge to help direct them, e.g. Can you see a circle in your eye? Can you see any curved lines or small dashes on your eyebrows?
- Proceed to guide the children through recording the shapes and lines they can observe on their faces – use proportional guidelines to help you. Guide the class as they simplify their facial features into shapes and lines. You could go to nose, mouth, ears then hair.
- When the children have copied the basic shapes and lines of their face, see if they can observe lighter and darker areas and add them to their drawings. Demonstrate how to use the side of the pencil to shade with. Remind the children that they can press harder to get a dark tone and apply less pressure for a lighter tone.
- You could stop the children nearer the end of the lesson and demonstrate cross-hatching. Allow the children a bit of time to add some cross-hatching to their portrait.

Plenary

Gather the children and have a class critique, looking at how well the children have recorded shapes and lines to represent their faces. Highlight where some children have managed to show light and dark tones and used cross-hatching, and encourage those children to remind the class how they achieved that. Remind the children that drawings include lines, shapes and marks, and sometimes we can add tone (light and dark areas). Ask the children if they noticed anything new about their faces as they were looking so closely.

Further activities

1. Lesson 1 could be extended by taking the children outdoors to make landscape drawings from direct observation using contrasting lines and marks.
2. You could have the children make their self-portraits from black and white photographs rather than from life.

Cross-curricular links

Maths: Make links with maths learning around shapes and shape drawing.
Science: Observational drawings of plants and other living things.
History: Observational drawings of artefacts or a portrait of a historical figure.
Computing: Children can use a drawing application to practise creating images using simple shapes and lines.

Cave drawings

In 30 seconds...

In these lessons, the children are introduced to cave art as the oldest form of art and so they begin to develop a notion of chronology in art. Through looking at the images from the Lascaux cave, the children learn about how people in the Stone Age lived and why hunting was so important to their livelihood. They create their own versions of the cave paintings using simple line and shape drawings of animals using a variety of materials. This should build on the drawing scheme and children should use their awareness of line and shape to create their animal drawings on the cave background.

Key artwork

Any image from the Lascaux cave paintings, preferably one which shows a range of animals (see Figure 1B for examples of the Lascaux cave paintings, and 1C and 1D for examples of children's work)

What do I need to know?

In 1940, while walking in an area of southwest France, four children and their dog made a remarkable discovery – they stumbled across prehistoric cave paintings. The Lascaux cave paintings, c.15,000–20,000 years old, depict a range of wild animals that were once native to that region of France. The cave itself has different sections, each room containing a selection of paintings and engravings of these large animals. Due to the damage being caused by excessive visitors to the caves, namely through the carbon dioxide produced, a replica of some of the cave rooms was opened and these copies of the caves receive many visitors annually.

It is estimated that the cave contains 2,000 images, mainly depicting large animals but also some symbols and one person with a bird's head. The animals shown in the various chambers include: bulls, stags, cows, horses, bison and even a rhinoceros. The techniques used were drawing, engraving and painting. The detail and sense of movement in these paintings is impressive even by today's standards; it is said that when Pablo Picasso visited the caves, he announced his disbelief at the level of sophistication in the Stone Age art. The drawings are made of simple lines and shapes yet they manage to capture the essence of the animals in a way that we associate with modern, skilled artists.

Painting in the Stone Age would have come with challenges, one of which was poor lighting. The caves are dark and the prehistoric artists would have worked using flames or lamps fuelled by animal fat, and they probably only worked for short periods of time. Impressively, archaeologists have ascertained that the Lascaux artists made and used a form of prehistoric scaffolding to reach the high walls and ceilings of the caves. Prehistoric life was tremendously far removed from the convenience we enjoy today, and embarking upon these paintings would have involved some planning and preparation, such as first making the utensils or paintbrushes with which to paint. Fingers, moss, horsehair and twigs are all tools associated with Stone

Age painting. It seems, from the remains of colour-stained hollow bones found at the Lascaux site, that a type of spray painting involving blowing paint through the bone tubes was used for larger areas of colour. Likewise, paints were made by hand from resources available in the immediate environment. The artists ground up coloured rocks and earth with spit, water, or animal fat to make their paint. We can see the limited colour palette that these minerals created when we look at the cave paintings. The artists often used the natural curves of the stone walls to accentuate the animal's physique.

There is much speculation about the purpose of this art and no one is certain, but the idea that these images were made merely for their aesthetic quality is widely disputed. The images are specifically of animals and they are in a dark cave and not readily seen. Some experts believe that the animal images are linked to visualisations that the Stone Age people created to subjugate the animals, a kind of wishful drawing. These could be related to hunting which was the mainstay of survival. However, many of the animals depicted are not those that were typically hunted. Other experts are convinced that the caves were used for spiritual ceremonies, the details of which are unknown.

Cave art has been found in Asia and Europe. 40,000-year-old cave art has been found in Indonesia. Cave art is one of the earliest forms of painting and drawing that we know of and it is evidence of our species demonstrating characteristics and behaviours that we associate with being modern human beings.

- The Lascaux caves are in **France**.
- Cave art is some of the earliest examples of art that we know of today.
- **Prehistoric** paintings inside the caves were discovered by French teenagers and their dog in 1940.
- The cave paintings are of animals that would have been found in that area at that time.
- The **Stone Age** artists painted, **engraved** and drew on the cave walls.
- The colours are limited because the paints were made from natural materials available at that time and in that area.
- No one is certain why these images were created in this cave, but some of the animals were **hunted** by prehistoric man.
- The pictures are made up of simple lines and shapes but they look as good as any drawings or paintings produced today.
- The brushes and paint used were made from **minerals** and resources found nearby.
- Picasso visited the Lascaux caves and he was impressed with the drawings.

Vocabulary

Engrave: To cut a design on a surface.
France: A country in Europe.
Hunt: To chase and kill an animal for food.
Mineral: A naturally occurring material.
Prehistoric: A time before recorded history.
Stone Age: A time in prehistory when humans used stone tools.

Useful links

www.lascaux.culture.fr/?lng=en#/en/00.xml Website for the Lascaux caves
www.visual-arts-cork.com/artist-paints/prehistoric-colour-palette.htm Information about paints made from natural minerals

Lesson 1 Cave wall

Key artwork

Any image from the Lascaux cave paintings, preferably one which shows a range of animals (see Figure 1B for examples of the Lascaux cave paintings, and 1C and 1D for children's work)

You will need

- A3 cartridge paper
- Chalks in red, yellow, brown, black, and white
- Table covering
- Aprons

Preparation

The children will be rubbing and smudging chalks across their paper to create a cave wall background; a table cover may be needed or a cloth handy to wipe up afterwards. Place a selection of chalks, in a range of natural colours, within easy reach of the children. You could also prepare your own cave wall on A3 paper – do this without scrunching the paper so that you can demonstrate the effect of scrunching in front of the children.

Getting started

Look at the key artwork with the children and discuss what they can see. Encourage the children to notice the different types of animals and what they are doing. Ask the children if they think that this painting was done on paper and encourage them to look closely to work out that the surface is rough like a cave wall. Explain that this is the earliest form of art and that it was discovered on a cave wall in Lascaux in France by people a long time ago, in the Stone Age. Bring the children's attention to the way that the cave artists used lines and shapes to draw the animals, and ask them if they can recall any other artists who use lines and shapes. Ask the children to share ideas about where paints came from a long time ago, i.e. did these artists go to the shops to buy paint? Why not? Tell the children that artists invented the first colours with natural minerals with a combination of soil, animal fat, burnt wood and chalk. Ask the children to list the colours they can see in the artwork and explain that the minerals made red, yellow, brown, black, and white.

Class activities

- Tell the children that they will begin their cave art by making a background like a cave wall.
- Show the children a piece of A3 paper and ask the children to come up with ideas for making the paper look more like a cave wall.
- Demonstrate how to use the side of the chalks to rub across the page.
- Show the children how to scrunch the paper up and then flatten it to look like a rough cave wall.
- Ask the children to explore what happens to the chalk when they rub it over the scrunched paper, i.e. it makes darker and lighter areas, a bit like tones.

Plenary

Gather the children with their cave backgrounds and look at good examples of cave walls. Recap the fact that cave drawings were the first artworks to be created and that the Stone Age people were making art before they could even speak. Ask the children what they think the next step will be in creating their cave art, i.e. drawing the animals.

Lesson 2 Cave drawings

Key artwork
Any image from the Lascaux cave paintings, preferably one which shows a range of animals (see Figure 1B for examples of the Lascaux cave paintings, and 1C and 1D for children's work)

You will need

- Children's artwork from previous lesson
- Thin sticks and twigs, enough for each child to use two or three – these will get covered in paint so you may want to rest them on paper towels
- Black and brown poster paint in palettes
- Printed images of a Lascaux cave painting on the board and/or on tables
- Aprons
- Table covers

Preparation
Cover the tables and fill the palettes with the black and brown paints, ensure that each child can reach a palette and a selection of twigs. Print out and, if you intend to reuse, laminate copies of the Lascaux cave art, making sure that the animals are clearly visible, make sure each child can see a copy from their seat.

Getting started
Recap the key artwork with the children and look at good examples of children's work from the previous lesson, highlighting examples where the children have created a good 'cave wall effect'. Ask the children if they can think of any challenges that the cave artists might have had, e.g. the darkness, not having tools or paint. Ask the children to think about what the Stone Age people might have used to paint with and explain they used twigs, their fingers, horse hair and plants. Explain that in this lesson, the children will add the animals to their cave walls and show them how to look at the animals as lines and shapes to make it easier to copy them. Show the children the twigs and sticks, and demonstrate how they can dip these into the paint and use them as drawing tools. Show them how they can use different parts of the twigs to achieve different effects, and ask them to focus on the outline of the animals rather than colouring the inside. Remind the children to look at the images provided to copy the animals.

Class activities
- The children can now use the twigs and sticks to draw the outlines of the animals onto their cave backgrounds.
- As you move around the classroom, speak to the children about whether drawing with twigs is difficult.
- Encourage the children to work silently, reminding them that Stone Age people did not yet use words like they do.

Plenary

Have a gallery walk: the children walk around the class, pretending to be cave people and viewing the work – if you have space, you could use masking tape to tack the work up around the walls. Ask the children to share which artworks they like and why, and see if they can identify different animals in each other's work. Ask the children to feedback about how they found working with twigs instead of brushes.

Lesson 3 Cave art

Key artwork

Any image from the Lascaux cave paintings, preferably one which shows a range of animals (see Figure 1B for examples of the Lascaux cave paintings, and 1C and 1D for children's work)

You will need
- Children's artwork from the previous lesson
- Images of the Lascaux cave painting on the board and/or on tables
- Chalk in browns and reds
- Charcoal
- Table covers
- Aprons
- Fixative

Preparation

Lay the children's work out on the table. Ensure the charcoal and chalk are easily accessible for all the children. Place the images of the Lascaux caves around the classroom and/or on the board so that the children can see examples of how the animals were shaded and coloured.

Getting started

Recap the key artwork with the children and discuss how it felt drawing the outlines with the twigs last lesson. Explain that this lesson, the children will be able to add the colour to their animals. Ask the children why they think there are only a few colours in the cave paintings and remind the children that there were no ready-made paints – the cave people made their own. Show the children how they can look closely at the images and then use the chalk and charcoal to complete their animals (see Figures 1C and 1D for children's work). Highlight the different types of dots and lines used and refer to previous drawing lessons about drawing with lines.

Class activities
- Allow the children to use the images of the Lascaux cave art and add the final details to their own work.
- Use the fixative or hairspray to coat the work after the children have left, this will stop it from smudging.

Plenary

Allow the children some time to view each other's work. Recap the key themes of the scheme and remind the children of the different skills they used. Show the children the virtual tour of the cave (https://youtu.be/2hiFqqqjTxQ).

Further activities

1. You could tape large pieces of paper to the underside of tables and have the children paint upside down as if in a cave.
2. You could have the children make their own paints using berries, beetroot, paprika, mud, ground charcoal and chalk. Mix these with oil or egg yolk.

Cross-curricular links

History: This could be a good chance to introduce children to prehistory.

Geography: The children could make a map of all the cave paintings that have been found around the world.

Science: The children could experiment with ways of making paint from natural materials.

2 Painting

Colours and painting

In 30 seconds...

The lessons that follow introduce the children to primary and secondary colours, and warm and cool colours. The lessons do not yet begin to ask the children to select or mix colours that match actual objects, but instead the emphasis is on the children exploring colour mixing and on organising groups of colours to create an effect or feeling. These lessons provide opportunities for the children to learn how to use the painting equipment as they use different types of brushes and paint for different purposes.

Key artwork

Henri Matisse, *The Dessert: Harmony in Red (The Red Room)*, oil on canvas, 1908

What do I need to know?

The use of colour in painting has historically been affected by different issues, such as the availability of materials as was in the case with prehistoric paintings, and the artistic conventions of the time, as in work by the old masters of European art. It was during the nineteenth century, around the time of the Impressionist painters, that colour in painting began to take on the vibrancy, movement, texture and effect that we recognise today. This change was largely due to the availability of synthetic paints, whereas in the past artists or their assistants would have had to laboriously hand-prepare colours. In the Middle Ages, egg tempera was the commonly used paint. It was a mixture of pigments or coloured powders mixed from ground up stones, plants or metals and egg. During the Renaissance, artists began to use oil as a mixing medium and this dried more slowly, allowing for more detail and sophistication. The nineteenth century synthetic colours however, were more varied, brighter and ready-made.

Colour in paintings can be used to literally record what the artist sees, but there are also techniques that painters use to suggest depth or distance, e.g. landscape painters often use warmer, darker colours in the foreground and cooler, lighter colours in the distance. Colour can also be used to represent emotion, as is the case with many of Vincent van Gogh's paintings.

We use the 'RYB system' when mixing actual paints, and this is the best way to teach young children about mixing primary colours to create the secondary colours. It is useful to know that colour mixing *digitally* uses a different system because it includes light and colour; *printing* uses a system called 'CMYK'. RYB is an abbreviation of red-yellow-blue, and these are the commonly used primary colours we speak about when teaching colour mixing using paint, i.e. the actual colours or hues in paint form. In theory, the primary colours are the origin of all other colours and they cannot be produced using any of the other hues. The primary colours can be described as the 'big boss' colours to young children. Three secondary colours are made when you mix the primary colours in groups of two, they are: orange, green and purple or violet.

Sir Isaac Newton developed the first circular diagram of colours in 1666, and there have been many adaptations since. The colour wheel is a useful tool for artists and can even be used to work out good colour combinations, i.e. complementary colours or analogous colours.

While there is no hard and fast rule about warm and cool colour groupings, it can be said that reds, oranges and yellows are 'warm' and blues, greens and violets are 'cool'. That said, yellow and violet are affected by their adjacent colours and can appear warm or cool depending on their surroundings. The key artwork by Matisse (*The Dessert: Harmony in Red*) is a good example of how a colour can dominate a painting and create an atmosphere; there is a clear contrast between the bold red room and the view of the painting or through the window. The children will be able to use their knowledge of the primary and secondary colours to identify familiar colours in the painting. They can also use their awareness of lines and shapes to describe this painting, such as the patterns in the room and items on the table.

The Henri Matisse painting gives the children an opportunity to 'read' art. Children will discover how a painting can tell a story without the use of words. They can speculate about who the lady was, based on her actions and her outfit.

- Artists paint with colour; paints come in different colours.
- A long time ago, artists had to make their own paints using materials found in nature such as ground up rocks or earth.
- Stone Age artists used natural minerals mixed with spit or animal fats; later artists used **Tempera** paint, which was pigment mixed with egg.
- When paints were **manufactured**, ready-made and synthetic, the colours available were brighter and more varied.
- Colour is sometimes used to make something look more realistic but it can also be used to show a **mood** or feeling.
- Another word for colour is **hue**.
- **Primary colours** cannot be mixed using any other colours but they mix together to make **secondary colours**.
- Warm and cool colours can be used to create different feelings in a painting.

Vocabulary

Hue: A colour.
Manufactured: To make something using machinery.
Mood: A state of mind or feeling.
Primary colours: A group of colours that cannot be created using other colours.
Secondary colours: Colours resulting from the mixing of two of the primary colours.
Tempera: A quick-drying paint made by mixing coloured pigments with egg and sometimes oil or water.

Useful links

www.bbc.co.uk/education/guides/zq7thyc/revision/6 Information about colour and science
www.colormatters.com/color-and-science Information about colour and science
http://youtu.be/yu44JRTIxSQ A great video about primary and secondary colours to show the children, with a catchy song
www.hermitagemuseum.org/wps/portal/hermitage/digital-collection/01.+Paintings/
28389/?lng=zh *The Dessert: Harmony in Red* (The Red Room), clear version

Lesson 1 Mixing primary colours

You will need
- A1 sheets of paper or rolls of paper to cover tables
- One sheet of A1 paper for you to demonstrate on
- Poster paints in the primary colours
- Large brushes
- Water pots
- Aprons
- A colour wheel

Preparation
Lay out the A1 paper so that the children can share one between two, place a blob of each of the primary colours directly onto the paper, in the centre so that each child can reach. Place the water pots and two brushes within easy reach of each child – this can be on the paper if needed. The paper will be disposed of after the lesson. Enlarge and print a colour wheel diagram to show the children during the plenary.

Getting started
Tell the children that artists often like to use paints and colour in their work and show them the three primary colours by holding up the poster paint bottles. Tell the children that these three colours are very special; explain that they are going to find out why these are such important colours, and ask some children whether they can guess what is special about the colours. Gather the children around for a demonstration and explain that the paint you are using is called poster paint. Squeeze blobs of the three primary colours out onto your large piece of paper and build excitement by checking if the children are ready to see what magic these three colours can do. Describe that you are going to mix some of the colours together – make sure that the children know what that means. You could ask a volunteer to come and select one colour to pick up with the brush, placing it onto a space on the paper, then ask another child to choose another colour to mix with the first. You could ask the children to guess what is going to happen. Show the children how to gently mix the two colours together to reveal a new colour. Note: It is better to add the darker colour to the paler one. Demonstrate how to wash the brush effectively without splashing and to check that it is clean. Continue like this until you have mixed all combinations of primary colours. Tell the children that these magic colours are called the primary colours, and they are special because they make new colours called the secondary colours.

Class activities

- Allow the children time to explore mixing the primary colours together. Don't be too rigid about what they are painting; this is more about the children using the equipment and exploring colour mixing.
- You could stop the children and set them colour mixing challenges, e.g. 'Who can make the secondary colour orange?'.
- Draw the class's attention to children who are remembering to use the equipment well, e.g. 'I like the way that Gabby remembers to wash the brush after she uses it.'

Plenary

Gather the children and recap what the primary colours are and which two are mixed to make each of the secondary colours. Also, highlight the great way the children used the paints, brushes and water pots. You could show the children the colour wheel and tell them that this is a good tool that artists use to remind them about the primary and secondary colours.

Lesson 2 Warm and cool colours

Key artwork

Henri Matisse, *The Dessert: Harmony in Red (The Red Room)*, oil on canvas, 1908

You will need

- Key artwork on the interactive whiteboard and printouts of it so that the children can see the key artwork while they work
- A slide showing warm and cool colours and printouts so that children can refer to them while they work
- Watercolour paints
- Thin brushes
- Water pots
- Aprons
- A4 worksheet with a small rectangle outline to serve as the window like the one in the key artwork (see **Bloomsbury Online Resource 2A**)

Preparation

Print copies of both the key artwork and the examples of warm and cool colours.

Getting started

Show the children the key artwork by Matisse, explain that he is an artist who used colour in his work. Ask them whether they think he used a pencil to make this picture and if not, what material did he use? Explain that this is not a drawing but a painting. Spend some time allowing the children to 'read' the image. Encourage them to extend their thinking about their responses, for example, if a child says that they see a lady, extend their thinking by asking what she is doing or wearing; if a child says they see a pattern, you could ask them to describe other places where they have seen patterns. Next, bring the children's attention to the fact that red is the predominant colour. Ask the children if they like it and how red makes them feel. Explain that artists often use colours to make us feel certain things; ask the children to imagine and describe how they would feel if they were standing in that red room. Explain that reds and oranges are supposed to make people feel energetic, whereas a colour like blue or green is supposed to make us feel calm – ask the children if they agree. Show the children the slide with the warm and cool colours presented then help the children to identify that Matisse has used mainly warm colours inside the room and mainly cool for the outside (some children might notice that this window could be seen as a painting in a frame – it is fine to say that as we can't tell for sure).

Explain to the children to that they will be using a type of paint called watercolour paints and ask the children to feedback how these paints are different to the poster paints they have used before. Ask the children why they think it is necessary to use such a small brush with these paints, i.e. they are small. Demonstrate how to hold the brush like a pencil, load the bristles of brush with paint, use the brush on the paper and wash it in the water pot.

Class activities
- Give the children their paper and show them the outline that you have made for the window, tell the children that this is like the window in Matisse's work.
- Ask the children to make their own painting that uses warm colours on the inside of the room and cool colours for the view out of the window (have warm and cool colours on display to remind the children).
- Explain that they might want to copy Matisse's work (have a copy in view) or use their imaginations or memories to design their own room and view.
- You could let the children use a pencil to draw their design first – however, painting directly with the thin brushes can work well too.

Plenary
Gather the children and recap what the warm and cool colours are. Have the children be art critics of each other's work, explaining where they can see warm and cool colours and how well the artist has used the paints and brushes.

Lesson 3 Imaginary landscape

Key artwork
Teacher's example (see Preparation in this lesson)

You will need
- A4 paper, one sheet each
- Pencils
- Watercolour paints
- Thin brushes
- Water pots
- Black felt tip pens
- Aprons

Preparation
Prepare two examples:

Create a line drawing of an imaginary landscape, using different types of lines in the background and foreground. For example, you could use lots of zigzag lines for a rugged mountainous foreground and then broad wavy lines for a background sky. Create a second example of the completed painting stage, i.e. the foreground painted using warm colours and the background painted using cool colours, or vice versa.

Set up the tables so that each child can reach a set of watercolour paints and a water pot. Have examples of the warm and cool colours visible for all the children, either as handouts or on the board (see **Bloomsbury Online Resource 2B**).

Getting started
Spend some time recapping with the children all that they know about different lines, mixing primary colours and the difference between warm and cool colours. Explain that they will be making a piece of work that uses all those skills.

Demonstrate how to use a pencil to draw different lines to create a foreground and a background for an imaginary landscape. Then show the children how they can paint within the lines that they have drawn by painting the outline carefully and then filling in the space inside. The idea is to select only warm colours for the background and only cool colours for the foreground (or vice versa). Encourage the children to mix their own secondary colours rather than using the ones provided for them.

Note: This could be spilt into two or more lessons with the drawing part as one lesson and the painting part as subsequent lessons.

Class activities
- Ask the children to use their pencils to draw the imaginary landscape lines – a foreground and contrasting background. Support them by using your example and reminding them about the different types of lines that they could use.
- Ask the children to paint within their lines, using only warm or cool colours for either the foreground or the background.
- Remind the children to try to mix the primary colours to make their own secondary colours.
- If there is time, the watercolours dry fast so the children could go over their pencil outlines with the black felt tip pens.

Plenary
Have a gallery walk: the children pin their work up around the classroom or just lay it out on the tables and then all silently view the gallery of the whole class's work. You could ask the children to stop at artwork they like and explain what they like about it using as many of the subject specific vocabulary from the drawing and painting schemes as they can.

Further activities

1. Another idea for Lesson 3 would be to have the children draw around their hand and create patterns inside and outside the outline. The children can then fill the inside of their hand with warm colours and the outside with cool colours.
2. The colour mixing lesson could be followed up by creating a water and food colouring mix of each of the primary colours, using clear plastic containers. The solutions can be poured into palettes and the children can use pipettes to create new colours in the empty spaces of the palette.
3. Colour mixing could also be done by mixing coloured play dough.

Cross-curricular links

Science: This could work well alongside a topic about Isaac Newton and how white light is composed of all the colours of the spectrum.

Science: Look at colours as they appear in nature, including natural pigments and spectacularly coloured animals and plants.

History: Study how paints were made in the past, where colours came from and what they represent.

English: The children could practise descriptive writing inspired by fantastical colours and colour combinations/the feelings created by colours.

Painting like Georgia O'Keeffe

In 30 seconds...

In these lessons, the children will be inspired by the work of Georgia O'Keeffe and they will experience making close observations of flowers to record them in detail. The children will take on the role of a bee exploring the inside a flower to give them the right perspective for this artwork. These lessons encourage the children to become aware of the size and shape of the surface that they are working on in order to fill the paper.

Key artwork

Georgia O'Keeffe, *Oriental Poppies*, oil on canvas, 1927

What do I need to know?

Georgia O'Keeffe (1887–1986) was an American artist, probably best known for her magnified flower paintings. O'Keeffe's work *Jimson Weed/White Flower No. 1* (1932) is significant as it is the most expensive painting by a female artist ever to be sold at auction – it sold for $44.4m in 2014. The themes that are frequently referred to in relation to O'Keeffe's enlarged flowers are often adult in nature, and the artist herself has distanced herself from some of the associations. Likewise, the artist rejected accolades for being a good *woman* artist and insisted that she was one of the best painters irrespective of her gender. Aside from their erotic nature, these flower paintings are appealing to young children as they capture the beauty of nature in a direct and accessible way.

O'Keeffe was born in Wisconsin to dairy farmers and knew from an early age that she wanted to be a painter. She studied painting with a local watercolourist, and her mother encouraged her artistic abilities. Later, she studied at the Chicago Institute of Art and she was involved in her first exhibition in New York in 1916. The work that she exhibited already demonstrated a unique style and a tendency to abstract and simplify her observations. In 1929, O'Keeffe travelled to New Mexico, which would later become her home and the landscape from which she drew the most inspiration; she eventually moved there permanently in 1949. In New Mexico, Georgia O'Keeffe led a relatively isolated life; she enjoyed the solitude, the light and the deserted landscape, taking long walks and painting.

For nearly 70 years, this artist produced paintings on a variety of subjects, including but not exclusively flowers. Some of her lesser-known works depict New York skyscrapers, shells and bones. O'Keeffe's work portrays her own emotional response to simplifying nature, usually in a way that had a striking visual outcome. She was one of the pioneers of abstraction.

O'Keeffe's flower paintings explore details, colours, shapes and textures as if seen from the perspective of a small insect. The key artwork depicts two large red poppies in a full composition that reaches the edge of the canvas. Although the poppies are large in scale, the artist has painted the petals showing the delicate contours and layers. It is said that Georgia O'Keeffe enlarged her flowers to inspire even busy people to stop and enjoy their beauty.

Georgia O'Keeffe had a long and successful career and was one of the few female artists to gain respect in 1920's America, which was then a male-dominated environment.

- Georgia O'Keeffe is best known for her **enlarged** flower paintings.
- Georgia O'Keeffe always knew that she wanted to be a painter.
- O'Keeffe was inspired by nature and landscapes; she made observations and then **simplified** them in her work.
- The enlarged flower paintings include lots of **detail** and they show the **textures** in the flowers.
- The key artwork composition is full and reaches the edge of the canvas.

Vocabulary

Detail: Small features that could be difficult to notice.
Enlarge: To make something larger.
Simplify: To make something easier to understand.
Texture: How the surface of something feels.

Useful links

www.tate.org.uk/whats-on/tate-modern/exhibition/georgia-okeeffe Tate Modern old exhibition information, including *Oriental Poppies*
www.georgiaokeeffe.net Information about O'Keeffe
www.youtube.com/watch?v=v7lawD38Qy4 O'Keeffe talking about her life and work

Lesson 1 The viewpoint of a bee

Key artwork
Georgia O'Keeffe, *Oriental Poppies*, oil on canvas, 1927

You will need
- A3 cartridge paper, one each
- Pencils
- Good quality faux flower heads (better for longevity), one for each child
- Simple diagram of bee pollination (see www.edenproject.com/learn/for-everyone/what-is-pollination-a-diagram-for-kids)
- Magnifying glass, one each or one between two
- Two example pieces made by you, see Preparation in this lesson

Preparation
Lay the flowers out on the table so that each child has access to a flower. Make two versions of a pencil drawing of a flower, one that fills the page and has details of shapes, etc. and one that is very small in the centre of the paper.

Getting started
Look at the key artwork and explain that is by an artist called Georgia O'Keeffe who liked to paint flowers. Spend some time looking at the key artwork with the children and discussing the work, ask the children to comment on the colours, lines and shapes they can see. Ask the children if they think the flower is a giant flower in real life and ask them to think about why O'Keeffe might have painted it so large. Use this O'Keeffe quote to explain why the artist painted the flower so enlarged – she wanted everyone to stop and enjoy the beauty of the flower:

'So, I said to myself – I'll paint what I see – what the flower is to me, but I'll paint it big and they will be surprised into taking time to look at it.'

Ask the children if they can think of any insects that might see the flower the same way the artist has painted it. Explain that bees that are busy pollinating might see flowers like this and use the diagram to show how pollination works.

Class activities
- Explain to the children that they will be making an enlarged flower painting like Georgia O'Keeffe's.
- Give the children access to a magnifying glass and ask them to spend some time looking closely at the flower on their table. Encourage the children to notice patterns, lines, shapes and colours.
- Ask the children to share anything they noticed about their flowers and tell them that when artists are painting something they look very closely at it so that their painting can look realistic.
- Ask the children to place the flower near the top of their paper, so that they can see it easily.
- Show the children your two drawing examples and ask them which one is more like O'Keeffe's work and how they can tell, i.e. the enlarged one is more similar because it fills the page and has lots of details.

- Tell the children their challenge is to use their pencils to draw the lines and shapes that they can see but they must enlarge the flower big enough to fill the page – they should imagine that they are a small bee inside the flower.
- Explain that it is best to apply light pressure to the pencil as they are drawing, just in case they make mistakes or want to change their drawing.
- Make sure that the children keep observing the flower as they draw, using the magnifying glass to include details, rather than drawing from their imagination.

Plenary
Gather the children for a class critique and encourage the children to share what they like about each other's work, e.g. where has the artist managed to fill the page and make a drawing that looks like the view of a bee?

Lesson 2 Painting the flower

Key artwork
Georgia O'Keeffe, *Oriental Poppies*, oil on canvas, 1927

You will need
- Children's drawings from last lesson
- Good quality faux flower heads, same flower from last lesson for each child
- Magnifying glass, one each or one between two
- Poster paints in palettes and access to spare palette space for mixing colours
- Medium-sized flat brushes
- Water pots
- Aprons
- Your example from last week painted, see Preparation in Lesson 1

Preparation
Fill the palettes to match the colours needed for the flowers, e.g. you may not need to fill all the palettes with all colours depending on the flowers that the children have drawn. Place water pots and two brushes so the children can share one between two. Paint half of your enlarged flower drawing from last lesson, leave the other half to use for a demonstration.

Getting started
Spend some time recapping the key artwork and reminding the children why O'Keeffe painted the flower in such an enlarged way. Explain that in this lesson the children will be using paint and colour on their flowers. Use your example and demonstrate to the children how to paint around the edges of the lines in the drawing first and then fill the space with colour. Bring the children's attention to how you can use the corners of the brush to make thinner outlines and then use the flatter side of the brush for filling bigger spaces. At this stage, the children might not be able to record the differences in shades, so it is fine for them to block in the main

colours that they can see instead of the lights and darks (we can come to tone and texture next lesson). The focus should be selecting the right colours and staying within the lines that they have drawn. Remind the children about how to load and wash the paintbrush efficiently.

Class activities
- After the demonstration, the children can begin to paint the colours onto their drawing.
- Remind them to use the different parts of the brush for outlines and filling in colour.
- Stop periodically to show good examples of artwork where the artist has stayed within the lines and painted in one direction.
- Remind the children how to wash the brush and check it is clean to prevent contamination of colours.

Plenary
Have a gallery walk: the children leave their work out on the tables and walk silently around the room to view the work as if in a gallery setting. Ask the children to comment on paintings that they think have gone particularly well. Encourage them to use full sentences and art vocabulary to describe what they like, e.g. 'I like the way that Marcus has painted the warm colours on his flower'.

Lesson 3 As small as a bee like Georgia O'Keeffe

Key artwork
Georgia O'Keeffe, *Oriental Poppies*, oil on canvas, 1927

You will need
- Children's paintings from last lesson
- Same flower from last lesson for each child
- Magnifying glass, one each or one between two
- Poster paints in palettes and access to mixing space
- Small, thin brushes
- Water pots
- Aprons
- Your painted example

Preparation
Have the children's paintings presented for a critique as soon as the children begin the art lesson – either all on one table or tacked onto a wall in the hall or the classroom. Prepare the palettes with the appropriate selection of colours and have the flowers and magnifying glasses ready.

Getting started
Gather the children around to have a critique on last lesson's work. Explain to the class that this will be the last lesson on their paintings and ask them to think about what they think

needs to be added. Tell them that they will be adding the details and the textures using smaller brushes. Explain to the children what the word texture means and tell them that artists use texture try to show how things would feel to make their paintings look more realistic. Ask the children to feel the different parts of a flower and use words to describe the feeling. Show the smaller brush compared to the brushes they used last lesson and ask why they think the brushes need to be smaller. Look at the Georgia O'Keeffe key artwork and bring the children's attention to how much detail O'Keeffe has included; explain that she did this by looking very carefully and pretending to be small like a bee. Use your example to demonstrate to the children how to use the thin brushes to add details whilst using the magnifying glass to observe closely, show how the thin brushes can also be used in different ways such as dabbing or dashing to create textures. Highlight how to carefully load the brushes so that the paint doesn't gather in a blob or cover the handle.

Class activities
- Ask the children to use their thin brushes like careful artists to add the textures and details by looking closely.
- Pause the lesson periodically to show good examples of detailed painting and use of brushes.

Plenary
Have a gallery walk: ask the children to generate ideas about good behaviour in a gallery; have the children leave their work out on the tables and walk silently around the room to view that work as if in a gallery setting. Compare the children's work to the key artwork, drawing attention to paintings that are a similar style to Georgia O'Keeffe and discussing how the work is similar, e.g. fills the paper, has all the lines and shapes that can be seen, includes lots of details and shows the textures of the flower.

Further activities

1. A similar project could involve collaging or felt making instead of painting the flowers.
2. The children could use photography techniques to zoom into actual flowers and photograph them close-up. They could then use their own photographs to paint from.

Cross-curricular links

Science: This could be taught alongside a topic on plants and insects. The children could compare scientific diagrams of flowers with the O'Keeffe paintings.
English: Children could practise descriptive writing or poetry inspired by the life of a bee.

3 Collage

Paul Klee

In 30 seconds...

The lessons that follow introduce the children to Paul Klee's Castle and Sun painting. The children are encouraged to 'read' the image, using their broadening knowledge of shapes and colours to speak about the painting. Through learning about the key artwork, the children understand that artists can use their memories of places plus their imagination to create a picture, i.e. paintings do not have to be of real things. The children will make their own artwork inspired by the theme of a remembered and imagined place and then simplify their idea into basic shapes and colours using the collage technique. Although the Klee work is a painting, its simple shapes make it a good inspiration for collage work. This scheme should also provide an opportunity for children to focus on composition as they work towards filling the A3 paper.

> ### Key artwork
>
> Paul Klee, *Castle and Sun*, oil on canvas, 1928 (see Figure 3A, and 3B and 3C for children's work)

What do I need to know?

Paul Klee (1879–1940) was a Swiss-German painter whose style is hard to categorise; he spanned different movements, including expressionism, Cubism and surrealism. Klee was born in Switzerland into a musical family; his father a musician and his mother a singer and Klee himself was a talented violinist. In his early childhood, Klee was interested in a career as a musician but as a teenager he realised that the field of music would not provide a suitable creative outlet for him. Although Klee's taste in music was traditional, his art was to be more explorative and innovative.

In 1898, Klee began studying art at the Academy of Fine Arts in Munich and although naturally talented at drawing, he worked hard to understand colour and improve his use of it in his work. Klee developed a keen interest in colour theory and, as well as painting, Klee wrote extensively about the subject – these *Paul Klee Notebooks* are considered important contributions to modern art. In 1911, Klee met Kandinsky who was a successful artist and would later become one of the most significant painters of abstract art. Kandinsky and his peers were an inspiration to Klee and helped him to develop his style. In 1914, when Klee visited Tunisia, he was inspired by the different colours and light there, and his work began to move away from direct representation into colour and abstraction.

The key artwork is made up of simple geometric shapes resembling toy building blocks. The children will be able to identify shapes and primary and secondary colours in the work, as well as different shades of some colours. The colours are predominantly earthy brick colours but the shapes are an assortment of colours, ranging from pale, pastel to bold and rich. The painting is mainly made up of straight lines but the sun stands out as a large circle, echoed by the red archway at the bottom of the painting. We can establish from the title that the painting shows a castle, perhaps one that Paul Klee had visited and remembered. The image has no shadows and the shapes occupy their own space with no overlapping, an effect easily achieved through collage. Each shape appears to have a thin white outline or space around it, this could be the bare canvas underneath; the style bears a resemblance to the placement of tesserae in a mosaic. Klee has signed his name and date in an unusual position, next to the sun.

- Paul Klee's family were creative; they were **musicians** and he was also a talented violinist as well as painter.
- Klee considered a career as a musician but he felt that as a **painter**, he would have more creative freedom.
- Klee was good at drawing but he was not so confident using colour so he worked hard to study colour and become better at using it.
- Klee's castle combines his **memory** of a place and his **imagination**.
- Klee's work has lots of simple shapes and colours in it which make it look like a **collage** even though it is a painting.

Vocabulary

Collage: Art made by cutting and sticking various materials.
Imagination: Using the mind to create new ideas.
Memory: Something remembered from the past.
Musician: A person who plays music as a profession or is very talented at playing music.
Painter: A person who paints as a profession or is very talented at painting.

Useful links

www.wikiart.org/en/paul-klee/ castle-and-sun-1928 *Castle and Sun*
youtu.be/xGIW93jLkxI
Demonstration of cutting simple shapes

Lesson 1 Imaginary places

Key artwork
Paul Klee, *Castle and Sun*, oil on canvas, 1928 (see Figure 3A, and 3B and 3C for children's work)

You will need
- A3 paper/card in various colours
- Black felt tips
- Pencils
- Your own collage example (see Preparation in this lesson)

Preparation
Use A3 paper and coloured paper and/or card to make a collage of a place or building using shapes.

Getting started
Show the children the key artwork and explain that is a painting by the artist Paul Klee. Ask the children whether they can spot any colours, lines of shapes they know. Guide the children into understanding how Paul Klee didn't make the castle look realistic but instead used simple shapes to make his painting. Explain how the artist may have once visited a castle that remained in his memory and then he combined his memory with his imagination to make this painting. Ask the children if they can remember any buildings they've seen and invite some children to share their experiences. Explain that the children will be making large drawings of their memories.

Class activities
- Ask the children to close their eyes and picture the place they most enjoyed visiting, it can be a building or a place. Ask them to try and recall as many of the shapes, lines and colours that they can.
- Give each child a piece of A3 coloured paper and ask them to try and draw the building or place as well as they can remember it, using the pencils first then going over the lines with felt tips.
- Try to encourage the children to use lines and shapes for their drawing.

Plenary
Gather the children to talk through their drawings and share their memories of the building or place. Show the children your example of a collage and explain that next lesson they will be producing something like this. Remind the children that Klee painted his work but tell them you want to try a different technique called 'collage'. Ask the children to feedback about how they think you made yours and tell the children that you cut and stuck simple shapes onto your work and this is what a collage is.

Lesson 2 Shapes to cut and stick

Key artwork
Paul Klee, *Castle and Sun*, oil on canvas, 1928 (see Figure 3A, and 3B and 3C for children's work)

You will need
- Children's work from last lesson
- Glue sticks
- Paper and card in a variety of colours
- Your own collage example
- Plastic shapes (borrowed from maths resources)
- Pencils
- Scissors
- Class set of A4 envelopes for storing loose paper

Preparation
Lay the scissors, glue, pencils, plastic shapes and a pile of different coloured paper out on the tables so that each child can reach them. You should also lay out a selection of plastic shapes that the children can use to draw around if needed. Have each child ready with their imaginary drawing from last week.

Getting started
Recap the key artwork with the children and bring the children's attention to how Klee used simple shapes instead of making his building realistic. Show the children your example and demonstrate how you cut and stuck shapes to fit your drawing. Remind the children that 'collage' is the word we use when we cut and stick materials to make art. Explain that the children will be using their drawings from last lesson as inspiration for their collage – they will cut and stick shapes onto the drawing. (See Figure 3B and 3C for examples of children's work.)

Class activities
- Demonstrate how to carefully cut shapes from the coloured paper and then show the children how they could also use the plastic shapes to draw around first.
- Be sure that the children know that they should snip not chop with the scissors and that they can turn the paper instead of their bodies to cut awkward parts.
- Demonstrate how to stick different shapes onto the drawings to make up the parts of the buildings and scene – be sure to show the children how to use the glue carefully so as not to coat the paper too much.
- Allow the children to cut and stick shapes onto their drawing; try to encourage them to look carefully at their work to select the shapes that best fit the drawing. Note: The cut shapes do not need to perfectly match the initial drawing.
- Children can store loose cuttings in an envelope until the next lesson.

Plenary
Regroup the children and, now that they have collage experience, bring the children's attention to how to maximise the space on a piece of paper by using all the 'scraps' for smaller or different shapes. You could also show the video in *Useful links* section (page 46) to demonstrate how to cut multiple shapes at once. Look at good examples of children's collaging, e.g. where they have managed to cut neat shapes and fit them into the form of a building or place.

Lesson 3 Collage

You will need
- Children's work from last lesson
- Glue sticks
- Paper and card in a variety of colours
- Your own collage example
- Plastic shapes (borrowed from maths resources)
- Pencils
- Scissors
- Children's envelopes storing loose paper from last lesson

Preparation
Lay the scissors, glue, pencils, plastic shapes and a pile of different coloured paper out on the tables so that each child can reach them. You should also lay out a selection of plastic shapes that the children can use to draw around if needed. Have each child ready with their imaginary drawing/collage from last week.

Getting started
Look at good examples of the children's work from the previous lesson and highlight where children have successfully fit cut shapes to form a place or building. Remind the children how they can cut a variety of shapes and sizes to fit, and show them how they can layer paper to cut multiple shapes at once. Encourage the children to use different colours and shapes in their collages (see Figure 3B and 3C for children's work).

Class activities
- Children continue to cut and stick shapes onto their paper to create their collage of their imagined place or building.

Plenary
Have a gallery walk: the children have the chance to look at each other's work and comment on the things they like. Ask the children to share tips for cutting and sticking, e.g. 'We can turn the paper to cut around shapes', 'We use dabs of glue on the back of the paper shapes', 'We try to use a lot of different shapes and colours'.

Further activities

1. A similar project could work with paint instead of collage and the children could use their colour mixing knowledge to fill the outlines of shapes.
2. The children could also use a computer programme to create shapes in various colours – they could use the copy, paste, rotate and resize tools to create their imaginary building or place.

Cross-curricular links

History: Link the creation of this image to the study of a historic building – children can combine observations and imagination to create their piece.

English: Descriptive writing or poetry inspired by the imaginary building or place – children could create sentences that describe the place depicted in their work.

Maths: Link to learning about shapes.

Computing: Use a drawing and painting application to create the image.

4 Sculpting

Andy Goldsworthy: Working with nature

In 30 seconds...

The lessons that follow present the children with sculpture as an art form and then extend their understanding to include the non-traditional materials used by Goldsworthy, a contemporary artist who makes site-specific sculptures using natural forms. The children's preconceived ideas about what constitutes art will be stretched, and they will be asked to make their own temporary sculptures using natural forms in a lesson that takes place outside.

> ### Key artworks
>
> Andy Goldsworthy, *Nettle stalks. Attached to the thorns of hawthorn trees. Calm, overcast, March, 2009* (see Figure 4A)
> Additional images of Andy Goldsworthy's work, including some of his pencil sketches

What do I need to know?

Andy Goldsworthy (born 1956) is often referred to as an environmental sculptor; he creates his art in and out of natural landscapes. Other terms used to describe Goldsworthy and his work are land artist, site-specific artist and installation artist. Goldsworthy photographs his sculptures and although the art is essentially in the process, due to the temporary nature of his work, these photographs are often the only lasting evidence and have appeared in exhibitions and publications.

For young children, presenting Goldsworthy's work as sculpture as opposed to more traditional sculpture is deliberately liberating. Goldsworthy's ephemeral work has a magical quality that captures the imagination and empowers children to create without limitations about preconceived outcome, an approach that children can lose as they become more self-conscious about creating. Goldsworthy talks about the importance of the process and responding to site-specific materials, the conditions on that particular day and the setting. Through creating with nature, he gains a different perspective and relationship with it; rather than passively observing landscapes by way of appreciating the natural world, he works within it, embracing its joys and challenges.

There is a playful quality to Goldsworthy's work and the way he creates – he works within a variety of landscapes, exploring the resources and using his intuition. He works with materials such as slate, snow, ice, leaves, twigs, branches and he often uses natural objects to sculpt with, e.g. cutting twigs with a sharp rock.

He often makes sculptures that teeter on the edge of collapse, as if they are living sculptures that strike a delicate balance between tensions.

- Andy Goldsworthy is a **sculptor** who makes **sculptures** with the natural environment.
- Goldsworthy's work is often **temporary**, apart from the photographs he takes of it.
- Goldsworthy uses **natural forms** that he finds in the **landscape** that he is working in.
- The sculptures that Goldsworthy makes often change, **decay** or collapse due to weather conditions or the natural qualities of the items used.

Vocabulary

Decay: To rot over time.
Landscape: An expanse of scenery.
Natural form: An object found in nature.
Sculptor: An artist who makes sculptures.
Sculpture: A three-dimensional form.
Temporary: Lasting for a short period of time, not permanent.

Useful links

www.bbc.co.uk/education/clips/zh4wmp3 Video of Goldsworthy working
youtu.be/vWcebVXNrDw Video showing a selection of work by Goldsworthy
Bloomsbury Online Resource 4A Nettle stalks. Attached to the thorns of hawthorn trees. Calm, overcast, March 2009

Lesson 1 Using nature to make art

Key artwork
Andy Goldsworthy, Nettle stalks. Attached to the thorns of hawthorn trees. Calm, overcast, March 2009

You will need
- A collection of natural forms, e.g. twigs, shells, leaves, pine cones, acorns
- A camera to photograph the finished sculptures

Preparation
Make a substantial collection of natural forms, enough for the children to work in groups and use at least four or five objects to make a sculpture. Lay out the natural forms on tables so that the children can select the ones they want to use. You will need containers to store the natural forms in so you can reuse them in the future.

Getting started
Ask the children to tell you all the different materials that they can think of for making art and explain to them that artists use these different materials to draw, paint and create collages. Explain that some artists like to make sculptures and that a sculpture is a type of art that can

be viewed from all angles – it is three-dimensional. Ask the children to name some materials that they know of for making sculptures. Ask the children if they have ever seen a sculpture and share some examples that your class might know, e.g. any sculptures in public spaces. Show the children the key artwork and ask if they think this is a sculpture and whether they know what it is made from and where it is. Explain to the children that Goldsworthy likes to use nature to make his sculptures and give them some background to the artist and his approach. Highlight the fact that Goldsworthy, unlike Picasso or Van Gogh from previous lessons, is alive – he is a contemporary artist. Show the children some of the items that you have collected and explain that they will be making sculptures out of them, working in groups.

Class activities

- Bring the children's attention to the items that you have set out for them and ask the children what they notice about the items, i.e. they are all found in nature.
- Explain that the children will be working in small groups to create a sculpture using the natural forms.
- Highlight the fact that there is no glue or tape and ask the children how they will join items.
- Demonstrate how the items can be balanced on top of each other and can be connected by placing them next to each other in different ways.
- Make sure the children know that the sculptures do not have to show anything in particular, e.g. a person or a house.
- Put the children into small groups and allow them time to create using the natural form objects.
- Take photographs of the children as they work and of the final work, or have them take the photographs themselves.

Plenary

Allow the children time to look at each other's creations and discuss how the process of creating with natural objects felt. Explain that, like Goldsworthy's sculptures, the children's sculptures are temporary and ask the children if they can work out why Goldsworthy's sculptures don't last. Tell the children that because Goldsworthy's sculptures are made in nature they are not long-lasting, and discuss reasons for this, e.g. the weather and decay. Tell the children that in the case of Goldsworthy's work, if it wasn't for the photographs, we wouldn't have any evidence of his sculptures. Allow the children to dismantle their sculptures and ask them to reflect on how it feels that their work is not permanent.

Lesson 2 Collaborating

Key artwork
Andy Goldsworthy, *Nettle stalks. Attached to the thorns of hawthorn trees. Calm, overcast, March 2009*

You will need
- A collection of natural forms, e.g. twigs, shells, leaves, pine cones, acorns
- An outdoor space where the children can go to make a sculpture – preferably with some potential for collecting their own natural forms such as leaves and twigs
- Something for the children to store their collections in, one between two or per small group
- A camera to photograph the finished sculptures

Preparation
Make a preparatory trip to the outdoor space that you will take the children to and ensure that it is safe for the children to scavenge for natural forms there. Upload the images from last lesson to your interactive whiteboard and have them ready to show the children.

Getting started
Display one of the photographs of the children's sculptures from last lesson on the interactive whiteboard. Ask the children whether they think this is art and discuss why or why not. Ask the children whether they think that the art is the photograph or the sculpture from last week. Recap how Goldsworthy's work is often temporary and therefore needs to be photographed otherwise there would be no evidence of it. Ask the children how they could make their work more like Goldsworthy's, e.g. they could make the sculptures outside. Tell the children that they will be working outside in small groups to make work like Goldsworthy, discuss any challenges they think they might face.

Class activities
- Take the children outside and give them some time to collect items (take your pre-collected items with you).
- Allow the children to work in groups or pairs to create a sculpture outside – supplement the items the children find with some of the additional natural forms from your own collection.
- Explain to the children that, like Goldsworthy, they will take photographs of the work as it will be temporary.
- Allow the children to photograph their work when it is finished.

Plenary
Take the children back in to the classroom and discuss the joys and challenges of working outside. Ask them to share anything they noticed about the materials that they were working with. Ask the children to discuss working outside compared to making the sculptures inside, and whether they preferred it and why. You could look at some more of the photographs from last lesson.

Lesson 3 Proposal of art for a public place

Key artworks
Examples of Andy Goldsworthy's work, including some of his pencil sketches (a simple internet search will find these).

You will need
- The photographs of the children's sculptures from the previous lessons, printed out so that the children can have a copy each (for their sketchbooks, folders or to take home)
- A range of Goldsworthy's works from an internet search including his pencil sketches, ready on the interactive whiteboard
- Paper and pencils

Preparation
Print the photographs of the children's sculptures for them to keep. Carry out an internet search to find a selection of Goldsworthy pencil sketches and other examples of his sculptures, print them or have them on a slideshow ready to share with the class.

Getting started
Share some more examples of the artist's sculptural work with the children and recap the key themes in Goldsworthy's work. Ask the children to share what they like about the pieces and which they prefer. Explain that sometimes artist's sketch their ideas before they make their sculptures; a sketch is like a drawing but a bit less neat and sometimes made faster. Tell the children that sketching is a good way of designing and exploring different ideas before making something, it gets ideas out of your head and into the world. Show the children some of Goldsworthy's sketches and discuss the ideas that the sketches are depicting.

Class activities
- Ask the children to make sketches of some ideas for sculptures using any natural forms they like, including materials that may not realistically be available, e.g. ice or lakes. Children could look at some of Goldsworthy's sculptures and sketches for inspiration.
- Encourage the children to make their sketches ambitious and in a setting of their choice, as these are ideas and not sculptures that they will be able to make.
- Ask the children to think about which materials they would like to use, e.g. ice or snow, and to think about the setting, e.g. what the background will be and where the sculpture would be built.
- Ask the children to jot down the variables that will influence the making of this sculpture and how long it will last in the setting, e.g. an ice sculpture will melt or the sea will wash a sand sculpture away.

Plenary
Regroup the children and ask them to share their ideas for the sculptures, including materials and settings. Encourage them to refer to their sketches as they describe their ideas and the challenges they think making the sculpture in that setting would bring.

Further activities

1. You could have the children replicate one of Goldsworthy's sculptures – select images of one that has been created using readily available materials such as autumn leaves.
2. Plan a trip to an inspiring natural setting and allow the children to spend the day creating in nature.

Cross-curricular links

Science: Make links with learning about plant and animal habitats.
Literacy: The children could create poems that describe their sculptures in the outdoor setting and the different materials they used.
Computing: The children could superimpose their sketches into their ideal setting, e.g. an ice sculpture at the North Pole.

Niki de Saint Phalle: Animal sculptures

In 30 seconds...

In these lessons, the children will use their prior experience of simple shapes to simplify a drawing and use it to build sculptures out of modelling clay. The children will look at a piece of public sculpture by Niki de Saint Phalle and learn how the inspiration for it was a Russian story. Using their own knowledge of fairy tales, the children will design and make an animal sculpture. They will learn how to manipulate the material to make basic three-dimensional shapes and they will use tools to join parts of the sculpture together.

> ## Key artwork
>
> Niki de Saint Phalle, *Firebird*, fibreglass and steel, 1983 (see Figure 5A)

What do I need to know?

Niki de Saint Phalle (1930–2002) was a French painter, sculptor and filmmaker. She was born in France and her family moved to America when she was a young child. As a teenager, she worked as a fashion model, and had photographs taken for publications such as French Vogue and Life magazine. In her twenties, she began experimenting with painting and creating works from found objects – she started to use art as an outlet for emotional distress and to aid recovery from illness. She eventually returned to Europe with her husband and daughter and, whilst travelling in Barcelona in 1955, she was inspired by various artworks, including the Park Güell designed by Gaudí. It is perhaps after this that she became interested in one day opening her own garden full of artworks, she began work on her sculpture garden named the Tarot Garden in 1980.

Niki de Saint Phalle was a self-taught artist, and her work in all mediums has a childlike and uncontrived quality – much of her work features flat, bold primary colours and has a make-believe quality. She said that her early works featured the same themes that she continued to work with throughout her life, and many of her first paintings contain fantasy creatures and fairy tale landscapes. Early on and again following a nervous breakdown, she created abstract relief pieces using broken items from around the house such as plates and toys, which were stuck in plaster to create a textured landscape. The best known of her early works are probably her *Shooting paintings* which she created by filling plastic bags with paint and other substances, and then shooting a rifle at the bags onto canvas. The result was as if the canvas had bled from the hole created by the rifle; the act of shooting itself was considered performance art.

Niki then began to explore themes around how women are portrayed and treated in society – she was concerned with not conforming to the typically female role that she saw demonstrated around her. At first the work inspired by this theme was confrontational and disturbing, but she soon shifted to a more celebratory approach and began to create sculptures such as *Nanas*. These sculptures are huge colourful and curvaceous women, often in triumphant and vibrant poses – they were intended to be displayed in public areas.

Many of De Saint Phalle's sculpture works are large-scale and displayed in public spaces, such as the key artwork, which is one of sixteen sculptures in the *Stravinsky Fountain* in Paris. This fountain was made in tribute to the composer Igor Stravinsky who made a famous piece of music called *Firebird*. The bird sculpture by De Saint Phalle is inspired by the firebird which also appears in a Russian fairy-tale. In the story, the bird is magical, glowing and hails from a faraway land. In 1981, the then mayor of Paris commissioned Niki de Saint Phalle and her then-husband Jean Tinguely to design the fountain. The fountain is a combination of two styles: De Saint Phalle's colourful sculptures and Tinguely's black mechanical sculptures. The firebird has holes in it to allow the wind to blow through the sculpture without blowing it away.

Children are naturally attracted to many of De Saint Phalle's sculptures because of their robust look and vivid colours. By using a fairy-tale character as inspiration for their sculpture, the children will already have a wealth of imagery available to them.

- Niki de Saint Phalle was a **self-taught** artist.
- She made art using all sorts of different **materials**; she was a painter and a **sculptor**.
- Niki de Saint Phalle made huge **sculptures** of **colourful** women called *Nanas*.
- The firebird sculpture was **inspired** by a character from a fairy-tale.
- The firebird is a huge **three-dimensional** imaginary animal.

Vocabulary

Colourful: Having lots of varied bright colour.
Inspire: To give someone an idea.
Materials: Things from which other things can be made.
Sculptor: An artist who makes sculptures.
Sculpture: Three-dimensional form.
Self-taught: Gaining knowledge and skill on your own, rather than through taught education.
Three-dimensional: Not flat (two-dimensional) and therefore appearing real.

Useful links

www.nikidesaintphalle.org/niki-de-saint-phalle/public-works *Firebird*
www.nikidesaintphalle.org Artist website
www.tate.org.uk/context-comment/video/tateshots-niki-de-saint-phalle Video about the artist
www.ilgiardinodeitarocchi.it/en Tarot Garden website

Lesson 1 Fairy tale animals

Key artwork
Niki de Saint Phalle, *Firebird*, fibreglass and steel, 1983

You will need
- A4 paper
- Pencils
- Colouring pencils or felt tip pens
- Several boxes of modelling clay in multiple colours (Giotto Patplume modelling material is a good choice)

Preparation
Source some images of animals from well-known fairy tales, such as the wolf from *Little Red Riding Hood* or *The Three Little Pigs* or the bears from *Goldilocks and the Three Bears*. Make your own sculpture design inspired by an animal from a fairy tale – use the bright colours available from the modelling clay pack.

Getting started
Show the children the image of the key artwork and explain that this is a photograph of a sculpture in a public space. Discuss with the children what a sculpture is and remind them of any previous sculpture work they have seen. Tell the children that the Niki de Saint Phalle sculpture is on show in a public space in France and explain to them how it forms part of the fountain which also has other sculptures. Ask the children what kind of animal they think this is; after a short discussion, tell them it is called a 'firebird' and it is a magical glowing bird from a Russian fairy tale. Tell the children that they will be making a small animal sculpture inspired by an animal from a fairy-tale they know. Mind map with the children any animals from well-known fairy tales that they know, and show the children the images you have found. Explain that the children will be using a drawing first to design their sculpture.

Class activities
- Ask the children to select an animal from a fairy tale, they could use the images you have prepared or use their imaginations.
- Ask the children to make a drawing of their character.
- Show the children the colours available to them from the modelling clay pack and have them add colour to their design – you could show the children your design as an example.
- The children can then add colour with felts or colouring pencils.
- Make sure that the children know that their design does not have to look like the illustration – they can use their imagination to enhance and change the design. Highlight this by referring to the De Saint Phalle sculpture.
- Encourage the children to make their design using simple shapes – ones that can be more easily moulded from the modelling clay.

Plenary
Gather the children and look at their designs. Ask the children to choose and talk about the designs that they like. Show the children the modelling clay and allow them to handle it, explain that this is what they will be using to make their sculptures.

Lesson 2 Making a three-dimensional form

Key artwork
Niki de Saint Phalle, *Firebird*, fibreglass and steel, 1983

You will need
- Children's sculpture designs from last lesson and your own design
- Several boxes of modelling clay in multiple colours
- Clay tools
- Aprons
- Pencils
- Black felt tips

Preparation
Prepare small pieces of modelling clay (about the size of a ping-pong ball), enough for each child. Have the modelling clay set out on tables, in various colours, and have the tools available for each child or one between two. Have pieces of paper or card (approximately A5) for the children to build their sculptures on.

Getting started
Recap the key artwork with the children and remind them that they have produced designs for their own animal sculptures. Explain that the children will have a chance to practise using the modelling clay before making their sculptures. Give each child their small piece of modelling clay and set them quick challenges of making a sphere, a small sausage shape (suitable for legs of animals) and a larger squatter sausage shape (suited to the body of an animal). Model how to make these shapes first. Next, show the children how to use the clay tools to join two pieces of clay together, i.e. ruffle the two ends of the clay that you need to join and then spread the clay across. Allow the children time to practise.

Class activities
- Show the children, using your own design, how to break their picture down into simple shapes.
- The children can draw these shapes over the top of their design in pencil or a black pen.
- The children can begin to make these shapes using the modelling clay, trying to match the colours with their design. Allow the children the freedom to deviate from their designs as they become accustomed to the modelling clay.
- Remind the children to stop from time to time and view their sculptures from all angles, reminding them that it needs to be 3D.
- Children should make their sculpture onto the piece A5 paper or card, for easy storage..

Plenary
Bring the children together and look at the work on the sculptures so far. Ask the children to share their top tips for and challenges with using the modelling clay. Look at the key artwork and show the children how the sculpture is smooth. Show the children how to smooth over the joins they have made to get this effect.

Lesson 3 Animal sculptures

Key artwork
Niki de Saint Phalle, *Firebird*, fibreglass and steel, 1983

You will need
- Children's sculptures and designs from last lesson
- Several boxes of modelling clay in multiple colours
- Clay tools

Preparation
Have the modelling clay set out on tables, in various colours, and have the tools available for each child or one between two.

Getting started
Recap with the children how to join modelling clay together and how to use their designs to inform their sculpting.

Class activities
- Children continue to make their animal sculptures, smoothing joins and viewing their sculptures from all angles.

Plenary
Place all the small sculptures on one table so that the children can gather around them. Invite some children to select a favourite piece and explain why they like it. Ask the children to explain where they would like to see their sculpture placed in their locality, so that members of the public can see it (imagining that it is a large version of the sculpture that they have made). Refer to the fact that Niki De Saint Phalle's sculpture is around a fountain in France.

Further activities

1. The children could make sculptures of human characters – you could guide them through making the body parts as a class to form one human shape.
2. You could dedicate a whole lesson to practising making different three-dimensional shapes.
3. The children could work in groups to make more than one character from well-known fairy tales.

Cross-curricular links

Science: This could be taught alongside a topic about animals or materials.
English: Descriptive writing or poetry inspired by the sculpture.
Computing: The children could photograph their final pieces and superimpose them onto an image of a public place, or you could use an animation program to bring the sculptures to life.

5 Printing

Collography

In 30 seconds...

Collography printing requires no specialist resources and the materials that you will need are easily sourced; it is a good way to encourage recycling. In these lessons, the children will experience using their own artwork as inspiration for making a collograph plate, and they will see how it is possible to interpret the same subject in different media.

Key artwork

An example of a collograph plate prepared by the teacher

What do I need to know?

While some printing techniques can be time-consuming and resource-heavy, collograph printing is straightforward and classroom-friendly. Building the collograph plate is much like creating a collage, the children will use one of their previous artworks as inspiration and rebuild it onto a plate. The more different textures that the children include, the more interesting their print will be. Be sure to glue all materials down well and allow to dry before printing.

- A **collograph** is a simple form of printing.
- Printing allows you to make more than one copy of your artwork.
- The artist must first make a plate to **print** from.
- The collograph plate should have a variety of **textures** on it.

Vocabulary

Collography (also spelled collagraphy): A printmaking process.
Print: A mark made on a surface.
Texture: How the surface of something feels.

Useful links

www.barbaragarrison.com/collagraphJumpPage.html Examples of collograph prints by an artist

Lesson 1 Designing a plate

Key artwork
An example of a collograph plate prepared by the teacher

You will need
- Children to have one of their pieces of art from a previous art lesson (one of these would work best: the shape drawing of an animal, self-portrait, imaginary place collage, enlarged flower. For ease, you could have all the children using work from the same previous topic, e.g. all use their self-portraits)
- A variety of items with different textures, such as:
  - Cardboard in different textures
  - Thick paper
  - Bubble wrap
  - Lollipop sticks
  - Foam tiles
  - Pipe cleaners
  - Tissue paper
  - String
- PVA glue and thick paintbrushes for gluing (brushes are better than spreaders for this as they reach in-between all the materials more effectively)
- Thick pieces of card to act as the collograph plate, cut to mimic the shape and proportions of the children's 'inspiration pieces'
- Printing ink – one colour will be sufficient unless you want the children to have a choice about the colour they use
- A printing roller
- A surface to roll ink onto, e.g. a smooth board or a tray palette
- A piece of paper larger than your collograph plate

Preparation
Ensure that all the children have access to a range of items with different textures and that they can use the PVA glue – place them within easy reach of all seats.

Prepare and dry your own collograph plate using the same 'inspiration piece' as the children will use – use materials of different textures to recreate the work on the thick piece of card. Be sure to paint the PVA glue over all the items, laminating them in.

Getting started
Explain to the children that they will be making a special type of art called a collograph print. Discuss different ways of making a print and find out whether the children have ever made a print in the mud, snow or sand; ask them what they used to make the print. Explain that printing means that we can create more than one copy of our art, a bit like the computer printer. Show the children your collograph plate and ask the children what materials they can see on it, allow the children to feel the surface of the plate and bring their attention to the fact that it has textures. Use your plate and demonstrate how to place a blob of printing ink onto the palette and roll it out until you hear a sticky sound. Roll the printing ink onto your collograph plate and then place a piece of paper over the top, gently rub the surface with your

hand so that you can feel the textures imprinting. Slowly peel the paper off the plate and reveal the print to the children.

Tell the children that printing takes a lot of careful preparation and you need to first prepare the plate to print from. Explain that they will start with one of their older drawings (or paintings) for inspiration – show the class your 'inspiration piece'. Explain that you used different materials to create the collograph plate and show the children how it is important to coat the items with glue, ensuring that the brush gets into all the spaces.

Class activities
- Show the children how to select different materials to make the image on their cardboard, forming a collograph plate.
- Ensure that the children coat the top of the items with glue as well as the underside.
- Allow the children the freedom to deviate from their drawing if they want to.
- Some children may find it easier to draw shapes onto the materials before cutting out or even to redraw the design onto the cardboard first and then cover it.
- Make sure that the cardboard and all the materials are totally laminated with the PVA glue and leave them to dry for next lesson.

Plenary
Gather the children and look at their work so far. Ask the children to share tips and suggestions with each other. Look at examples where children have used different textures and explain how that will create an interesting print.

Lesson 2 Collography

Key artwork
An example of a collograph plate prepared by the teacher

You will need
- The children's collograph plates begun last lesson (ensure these are completely dry)
- A variety of items with different textures, such as:
  - Cardboard in different textures
  - Thick paper
  - Bubble wrap
  - Lollipop sticks
  - Foam tiles
- PVA glue and thick paintbrushes for gluing
- Large crayons for rubbing over the collograph plates
- Pieces of paper larger than the children's collograph plates, thin newsprint paper works best

Preparation
Lay the materials out on tables so that all children can reach, as in the previous lesson.

Getting started
Recap the previous lesson with the children, focusing on how to use different textures to create an interesting print. Show the children how they can check how their print will look by placing the thin paper over their plate and rubbing a crayon over the top (it is best to hold the crayon on its side).

Class activities
- Give the children the crayons and have them 'test' their collographs by making a paper and crayon rubbing.
- Let the children discuss the results with the person next to them and make decisions about areas that they need to focus on.
- Allow the children to continue to build their collograph, adding more materials and coating with glue.
- Place the collographs somewhere to dry, ready for printing next lesson.

Plenary
Gather the children to recap the printing process using your collograph plate, ready for the children to print next lesson. Explain that important it is to wait for the ink to make a sticky sound; this indicates that there is the right amount of ink. Demonstrate how to make sure that the ink covers all the plate, carefully place the paper and then how to gently rub all over the paper with their fingertips then gently peel the paper off.

Lesson 3 Printing

You will need
- Printing inks
- Printing rollers
- Surfaces to roll ink onto such as a smooth board or a tray palette
- Pieces of paper larger than the children's collograph plate
- Aprons

Preparation
Set the classroom up ready for printing – cover tables with newsprint or plastic covering. Place ink trays on surfaces so that each child can reach one along with a roller and a pile of paper larger than the collograph plates. This lesson works well with the equipment set up one between two. Place a walnut sized blob of printing ink onto the top of each tray or surface. The children will need a space in the classroom to place their wet prints as they make them.

Getting started
Ask the children to write their name on at least three pieces of paper each (depending on how many prints you expect them to make) – this will be where they make their prints and it is easier to write names before the paper gets wet. Explain to the children that they will need to work in pairs to make their prints, supporting each other as they go through the process.

Class activities
- Let the children proceed through the printing process as you walk around and supervise.

Plenary
Gather the children with their favourite print and have a class discussion about what makes a successful print – why do some prints work better than others? Explain that there are different ways of making prints, and ask the children if they have ever made a print anywhere else, e.g. in snow or mud.

Further activities

1. The children could work in pairs on a larger collograph of a landscape or an abstract piece.
2. You could use found materials and ask children to collect their own materials from home to recycle them into art.

Cross-curricular links

Geography: The children could use the collograph method to create a print showing soil layers.

Part 2
Lower Key Stage 2

What does the KS2 curriculum say?

Pupils should be taught:

- to create sketchbooks to record their observations and use them to review and revisit ideas
- to improve their mastery of art and design techniques, including drawing, painting and sculpture with a range of materials [for example, pencil, charcoal, paint, clay]
- about great artists, architects and designers in history.

Curriculum content

The lower KS2 schemes are not divided so distinctly into the skill areas as the KS1 ones were, but are instead defined by the key artwork and practical outcome. They do still cover one or more of the same skill areas – drawing, painting, collage, sculpting and printing – and they will certainly extend the children's aptitude in them. By the end of lower KS2, the children should be using and controlling materials in a way that is distinctly more advanced than KS1 children. There are opportunities for using sketchbooks or paper for preparatory work.

The schemes in lower KS2 introduce the children to the concept of creatively interpreting the world around them and using popular culture as inspiration for their art. They will learn how other artists have done the same over the years. They will learn how artists can sometimes be radical and change the status quo to create new movements such as Impressionism, and how cultures around the world have and do create notable art.

The KS2 schemes continue to support children as they begin to make richer references to well-known artworks, through their own making and discussions and using subject-specific vocabulary. As the children progress through lower KS2, they should be given chances to have more in-depth discussions about artworks and they ought to be beginning to confidently speak about the formal elements (line/shape/tone/colour/composition/texture/space) in their own artwork and that of others. The teacher may begin to incorporate elements of literacy and written exercises into art lessons.

6 Fernand Léger: Drawing and painting

In 30 seconds...

These lessons introduce the children to the work of Fernand Léger (1881–1955). The children analyse his painting **The City** *and are introduced to how the artist abstracted a view of familiar imagery and conveyed a strong sense of a place through his work. The children will consider their local area and how it might be interpreted by a visitor. They develop a collection of semi-abstract images that represent their locality, and make their own artwork by fragmenting, overlapping and juxtaposing them in the style of Léger. This is a drawing and painting topic; the children will use their prior knowledge of simplifying images using lines and shapes as well as their colour-mixing skills.*

> ### Key artwork
>
> Fernand Léger, *The City*, oil on canvas, 1919

What do I need to know?

Fernand Léger (1881–1955) was a French sculptor, painter and experimental filmmaker who trained and began his career as an architect. Aged 25, Léger began to practise as an artist and was first influenced in style by the Impressionists. In 1907, Léger visited a Paul Cezanne exhibition and, influenced by Cezanne and others working at that time, his work began to take a semi-abstract Cubist approach that continued to develop into his distinctive style.

In 1914, Léger served as a soldier for the French army during the First World War. His experiences on the front line had an influence on his work and style. He began to paint machinery resembling artillery, and many of the figures that he painted at this time are made of cylindrical forms and have a monochrome robot-like quality to them.

Léger would regularly work with bold black, white, primary and sometimes secondary colours. He focused on striking geometric shapes and forms in his paintings. His compositions frequently depict a harmonious relationship between humans and the machines of industrial civilisation. His paintings do not necessarily hold a narrative, but the rhythms of the settings can be felt through his dynamic compositions.

The key artwork is a large painting made after the First World War. There are figures in the centre that could be soldiers returning from the front line. The image has many primary and secondary colours in it that children will find easy to identify. The imagery includes buildings, scaffolding, and bridges with other signs of city life such as shop window mannequins, plumes of smoke, and a telegraph pole. In *The City*, Léger is demonstrating the aptitude of Cubism to capture the vitality of city life. Léger was excited by the onset of a more mechanised way of life and he believed that modern city life would be improved by the Industrial Revolution. The artist's initials are hidden in billboard-style writing in the painting.

- Léger's work includes many vibrant primary and secondary colours.
- The key artwork represents modernity 'taking over' the city of Paris at the time of the **Industrial Revolution**.
- The key artwork **juxtaposes** buildings, scaffolding, and bridges with other signs of city life such as shop window mannequins, plumes of smoke, and a telegraph pole.
- The artist has used individual images which are fragmented and overlapping.
- The key artwork shows a **semi-abstract** view of the city.
- Léger embraced the **Cubist** idea of breaking objects into **geometric forms and shapes**.
- The key artwork evokes the sounds, smells, movements and sights of the city.
- Léger's work makes your eyes move around like they would on a busy street corner.
- The artist's initials are hidden amongst the colours and shapes.

Vocabulary

Cubist: A style whereby diverse views of the subject (usually objects or figures) come together in the same picture, resulting in images that appear fragmented and abstracted. Invented in around 1907/08 by artists Pablo Picasso and Georges Braque.
Geometric forms: Three-dimensional shapes such as cylinders and pyramids.
Geometric shapes: Made of regular lines, shapes such as squares, triangles, or rectangles.
Industrial Revolution: The development of industry that occurred in the late eighteenth and nineteenth centuries, brought about by the introduction of machinery.
Juxtapose: To place subjects together or close by for contrast or comparison.
Semi-abstract: The subject remains recognisable although the forms may be stylised.

Useful links

www.philamuseum.org/collections/permanent/53928.html?mulR=1671716044|3 *The City*
youtu.be/tOvnQ9Vqptw *Ballet mécanique* (1924). A post-Cubist art film conceived, written, and co-directed by Léger

Lesson 1 What Léger did, fragments of my locality

Key artwork
Fernand Léger, *The City*, oil on canvas, 1919

You will need
- Key artwork on a slideshow with the title and artist's name hidden initially
- Scrap paper or sketchbooks for mind mapping, one between two
- A3 cartridge or watercolour paper, one each

- A selection of images depicting the children's local area
- Pencils
- Eraser

Preparation

Prepare your own abstract pencil drawing that combines your memory of the sights and sounds of the local area and the images of the area. Be sure to overlap, use juxtaposition of images and have the images presented from different angles. A good way to achieve a similar style to Léger is to keep turning the paper as you work on the image, so that the drawing has no obvious 'right way up'. Source images of the local area, these could be whole pictures or fragments of pictures, you could also provide familiar symbols, road signs and street markings.

Getting started

Show the children the key artwork and ask them to discuss what they think they can see, ask them to describe the style. A good entry point could be to list colours and shapes, then move on to trying to work out what the abstract images are of. When the children have shared their initial perceptions and opinions of the image, bring their attention to the title of the work and ask them whether this gives them any further clues as to what the images in the painting are. Ask the children to look at the name of the artist too and to guess what nationality he was by looking at the letters, i.e. the accent on the 'é'. See if this gives them further clues as to where the painting is set. Share some of the information about the key artwork and then explain that the children will be making their own abstract image. Tell the children they will be using their own local area as inspiration and show them the images that you have collected.

Class activities

- Ask the children to create a mind map (either as a class, in pairs or individually) of some of the sights, sounds and smells of their local area. Also, ask the children to add any symbols and street signs that come to mind – they can use images and/or words for this.
- Ask the children to try to include their personal experiences of the area, e.g. the sounds in the local fish and chip shop or the architecture of the supermarket they regularly visit. Explain that they do not need to draw a full illustration but can simplify these ideas into simple drawings or symbols.
- Demonstrate to the children how to use their ideas plus the resources provided and begin to sketch out their artwork. Emphasise how they can overlap images and even select parts of the images to simplify and create the abstract style.
- Give the children their A3 sheet of paper and the image resources that you have prepared and let them begin to draw with their pencils – it is fine for them to use an eraser to refine their designs as they go.
- Encourage the children to keep turning their paper around as they add new drawings, to add to the abstract style.

Plenary

Bring the children together and look at their drawings so far. Highlight good examples of abstraction and overlapping, and ensure that the children understand how to achieve this.

Fig. 1A: Vincent van Gogh, *Fishing Boats at Saintes-Maries-de-la-Mer*, reed pen and ink, 1888

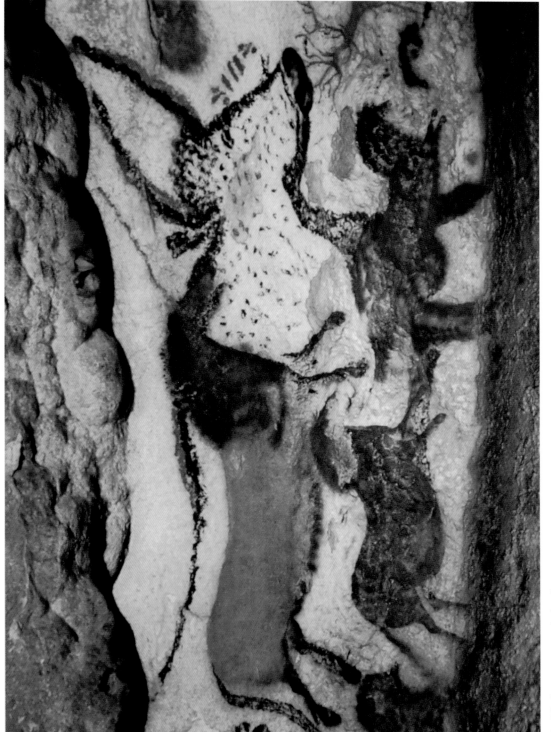

Fig. 1B: *Lascaux cave painting, France*

Fig. 1C: KS1 cave art example

Fig. 1D: KS1 cave art example

Fig 3A: Paul Klee, *Castle and Sun*, oil on canvas, 1928

Fig. 3B: KS1 Paul Klee collage

Fig. 3C: KS1 Paul Klee collage

Fig. 4A: Andy Goldsworthy. *Nettle stalks. Attached to the thorns of hawthorn trees. Calm, overcast, March 2009*
© Andy Goldsworthy

Fig. 5A: Niki de Saint Phalle, *Firebird*, Fibreglass and steel, 1983

Fig. 7A: James Rosenquist, *President Elect*, oil on Masonite™, 1960-61/1964

Fig. 7B: Lower KS2 Rosenquist pop art

Fig. 7C: Lower KS2 Rosenquist pop art

Fig. 11A: Katsushika Hokusai, *The Great Wave Off Kanagawa*, woodblock print, 1830–1833.

Fig. 11B: Lower KS2 printing local landmarks

Fig. 11C: Lower KS2 printing local landmarks

Fig. 12A: Richard Sweeney, *O3M (Shell)*, watercolour paper, 2010.

Fig. 12B: Lower KS2 paper sculptures

Fig. 12C: Lower KS2 paper sculptures

Fig. 21A: Willem Kalf, *Still Life with Drinking Horn*, oil on canvas, c.1653

Fig. 21B: Upper KS2 still life painting

Fig. 21C: Upper KS2 still life painting

Fig. 25A: Sarah Eisenlohr, *Settlers*, collage, 2012

Lesson 2 Selecting colours to evoke a mood

Key artwork
Fernand Léger, *The City*, oil on canvas, 1919

You will need
- Key artwork on a slideshow
- The children's drawings from the previous lesson
- A selection of images depicting the children's locality – these could be whole or fragments
- Pencils and erasers
- Watercolour paints and thin and medium-sized brushes
- Water pots
- Colour wheels or colour recipes (primary and secondary colours)
- Scrap paper for testing colours
- Aprons

Preparation
Prepare by painting a section of your own abstract drawing from last week – leave some unpainted so that you can demonstrate the painting technique in front of the class. Try to use similar colours to Fernand Léger and create your own colours rather than using the premixed colours.

Getting started
Give the children a chance to recap the main points about the key artwork and guide the discussion to focus more on the colours used. Explain that in this lesson the children will continue to complete their drawings and then start to add colour with paint. Gather the children around the demonstration area and use your own example to show them how to paint around the edges of the lines of their drawing first and then fill the colour inside. Show the children the selection of brush sizes available and ask them to feedback about why they might need different sized brushes for. Ensure that the children recall how to mix secondary colours and encourage them to mix their own colours rather than using the ready-made colours – it could be useful to have colour wheels handy for the children to refer to.

Class activities
- The children can continue to develop their drawing until they have a composition that they are happy with.
- The children can begin to add colour to their work, using the Fernand Léger image and colour wheels for reference.
- It is fine for the children to add pencil details as they paint, developing the composition as they go.

Plenary
Bring the children together and look at their paintings so far. Highlight good examples of abstraction, overlapping and painting. Ask the children to share their views on each other's

work and whether the pieces are beginning to evoke feelings of their local area. Look at the key artwork and bring the children's attention to the shades and tints in *The City*; demonstrate to the children how they can add small amounts of black to an original colour to make it darker, i.e. to create a shade. Show the children how to make an original colour lighter by adding white, to make a tint.

Lesson 3 This semi-abstract area of mine

Key artwork
Fernand Léger, *The City*, oil on canvas, 1919

You will need
- Key artwork on a slideshow
- The children's artwork
- A selection of images depicting the children's locality – these could be whole or fragments
- Watercolour paints and brushes
- Water pots
- Scrap paper for testing colours
- Aprons

Getting started
Gather the children around the demonstration area with their artworks and have a class critique, highlighting strong examples of abstract images, overlapping and colour mixing. Again, highlight the works that are beginning to evoke the atmosphere of the local area.

Class activities
- Allow the children time to look at their work and set targets for completion – this could be on sticky notes or on the back of the work.
- Allow the children time to continue to paint their work.
- Challenge the children to hide their initials somewhere in the painting.

Plenary
Have a gallery walk or a pop-up exhibition where the children share views on each other's work. They should try to use subject specific vocabulary and refer to the key artwork and how their work is similar/dissimilar to it. You could have children stop in front of their favourite artwork and explain to the class why this piece has caught their attention.

Further activities

1. Before sketching, you could take the children out for a walk with cameras to collect their own images of the local area.
2. The children could collect images of the area and combine these with their own photographs to create a collage.
3. The children could work on designing their own symbols for local landmarks, and then include them in their final design.

Cross-curricular links

Computing: The children could use computer editing programmes to layer and juxtapose their images, instead of painting and drawing. The children could make the image on the computer first and then use this as a plan to draw and paint from.

Literacy: This could form part of a topic around poetry or writing inspired by the locality.

Geography/History: The children could create the artwork inspired by research into a particular city or place.

7 Rosenquist pop art: Drawing, collaging and colouring

In 30 seconds...

In these lessons, the children will look at James Rosenquist's work titled **President Elect.** *They will replicate Rosenquist's technique of selecting images from popular culture to create a collaged source image and develop that into a final pop art piece.*

Key artworks

James Rosenquist, *President Elect*, oil on Masonite™, 1960–61/1964 (see Figure 7A, and 7B and 7C for children's work)
Preparatory collage for *President Elect*, easily found by adding 'collage' to a google search of the key artwork

What do I need to know?

James Rosenquist (born 1933) is an American artist who is known as one of the leading members of the pop art movement. Rosenquist was born in North Dakota and one of his first jobs aged 17 was as a sign painter in the Midwest, which led to work in New York, such as billboard painting in Times Square. Rosenquist used the money he made to train as an artist, and he often kept leftover paint to make his own work with. By 1959, Rosenquist was well known as a successful sign painter in New York. These billboard painting jobs were dangerous, and some of Rosenquist's peers were killed on the job, so with that in mind Rosenquist left the profession in 1960.

The billboard painting proved useful training for Rosenquist's subsequent pop art work and there are obvious visual links. Much of Rosenquist's work makes statements about American popular culture, using simple but powerful imagery in a bold advertising-like style. His work is large-scale like the billboard paintings that he started with, and it highlights issues to do with war, politics, consumerism and pop culture by taking fragments of images from these fields and combining them in paintings that represent contemporary life.

Rosenquist used abstraction and use of colour, texture, form and line to create multi-images that are expertly blended together. The images have the signature bold colours of pop art yet are distinctly his own style. Rosenquist made preparatory collages from original advertisements and magazine clippings; these give us an insight into his techniques and thought processes and are now considered works of art.

- James Rosenquist is considered part of the **pop art** movement.
- The creation of the key artwork began with a **preparatory** collage.
- The key artwork is similar in style to Rosenquist's **billboard** paintings of his early career.
- Rosenquist has used images from American **popular culture, advertising** and a portrait from the then presidential campaign.
- The style is unique in the way that it blends three images together to form one composition.

Vocabulary

Advertising: Calling the public's attention to a product or service, e.g. via television, newspapers, magazines, radio, the Internet, billboards, posters, endorsements, etc.

Billboard: A large outdoor board for displaying advertisements – billboard designs are more frequently made using graphic reproduction now, but historically they were hand-painted.

Pop art: An art movement that was extremely popular in the 1960s in America and Britain. Pop artists get inspiration from popular and commercial culture such as advertising. Other pop artists include Andy Warhol, Claes Oldenburg, Roy Lichtenstein, Peter Blake and David Hockney.

Popular culture: Activities, interests or products suited to the mainstream tastes of the masses.

Preparatory: Done to get ready for something.

Useful links

www.youtube.com/watch?v=14HFM3sucRE A video about Rosenquist
www.tate.org.uk/learn/online-resources/glossary/p/pop-art Information about what pop art is
www.guggenheim.org/arts-curriculum/topic/collage-and-scaling-up *President Elect* artwork
www.youtube.com/watch?v=DhEyoDCTSDQ What is pop art?

Lesson 1 Rosenquist's preparatory technique

Key artworks
James Rosenquist, *President Elect*, oil on Masonite™, 1960–61/1964
Preparatory collage for *President Elect*

You will need
- Key artworks on a slideshow – including a slide that shows the Rosenquist collage next to the painting, for comparison (or both images on a worksheet so the children can make the comparison)
- Whiteboards and pens
- A3 cartridge paper – one each for drawing
- A4 photocopy paper, for the preparatory collage
- A large collection of images and lettering taken from popular packaging, e.g. parts of cereal boxes or juice boxes (enough for each child to use at least three of the images each)
- Pencils and erasers
- Masking tape

Preparation

Gather a collection of packaging from well-known food products or consumer products; this should just be the section of the packaging that shows recognisable lettering or a logo. Use three or more of the parts of packaging to create your own preparatory collage by using the masking tape to attach them to the A4 paper, and lay them out in a composition that you will be happy to develop for a painting. Make a drawing of the preparatory collage on A3 paper; you will need to enlarge the collage and embellish by repeating parts and adding a background (see Figure 7B and 7C for children's work and the key artworks (Figure 7A) for examples). Be sure that you enlarge the images and superimpose, merge and juxtapose to make a composition that fills the A3 paper well.

Getting started

Show the children the painted version of the key artwork and ask them to describe what they see; they could list colours and items to start with and try to work out where the artist took the images from, ask the children if they think there are any links between the images or if they remind them of anything. Explain what the term pop art means and explain how this type of work uses popular imagery from the time it was made. Explain how Rosenquist used the portrait from the presidential campaign and ask the children to think about popular characters from contemporary politics and/or celebrities that might appear on art like this, if it were made now. Ask the children to create mind maps on the whiteboards with drawings and words to describe popular logos, packaging and celebrities – explain that these images are all from contemporary popular culture and that if the pop artists were making work today these images might appear in their work. Explain that the class will be making their own pop art using images from popular culture.

Class activities

- Point out to the children how large the painting is and then show the children the slide of the source collage. Look at and discuss how Rosenquist used this collage and then scaled it up or enlarged it to make the painting.
- Ask the children to compare the two images using the slide or a worksheet with the two images, and discuss how Rosenquist changed the source collage, in addition to scaling up, i.e. how has he joined the images?
- Scatter the images that you have sourced so that each child can access a range and allow them to select three to tape to their A4 paper as a preparatory collage.
- Show the children how to use the collage as a guideline for their A3 paper drawing, enlarging the images onto the A3 paper whilst making design decisions about how to merge the images and fill the spaces in-between. Use your work as an example.
- Let the children work on their drawings, using their A4 collages and the Rosenquist image as a reference for the A3 drawing.

Plenary

Draw the children's attention to the joins between the images on Rosenquist's work, and look more closely at how the artist has merged parts of the images, used a fading technique and blended gradients of colour to fill spaces in-between the images. Ask the children to think about how they might use some of these techniques or others to join their images together.

Lesson 2 Enlarging and creating a composition

Key artworks
James Rosenquist, *President Elect*, oil on Masonite™, 1960–61/1964
Preparatory collage for *President Elect*

You will need
- Key artworks on a slideshow and/or a handout
- Children's A3 artwork from the previous lesson, including their preparatory collages
- A large collection of images and lettering taken from popular packaging, e.g. parts of cereal boxes or juice boxes (so the children can refer to these for additional ideas about how to merge their three main images)
- Pencils and erasers
- Good quality felt tips
- Colouring pencils
- A colour wheel

Preparation
Use your own artwork example and
add some colour to it using the felt tips and colouring pencils – be sure to use the colours in way that creates a bold and eye-catching effect, like Rosenquist's work. You should also to use some of the methods for joining the images, e.g. blending and overlapping. Try to use complementary colours next to each other. Set the materials out on tables so that the children can easily select what they need.

Getting started
Explain that the next step is to add colour to the drawing, and look again at the use of colour in the key artwork. Highlight how during the pop art movement colours often appeared this bold style, mimicking the style of advertisements. Show the children the colour wheel and explain how complementary colours are colours that go well together and that they appear opposite each other on the colour wheel. Tell the children that people who design packaging often place complementary colours together and ask if the children can look at the colour wheel and then think of any examples of packaging which demonstrates use of complementary colours. Show the children how to colour around the lines of their drawing first and then fill in the space, colouring in one direction and leaving no white gaps. Look again at the areas where two images are merged, and encourage the children to consider how they will merge their images, e.g. with a rainbow design like Rosenquist's. (See Figure 7B and 7B for children's work.) Explain that because felt tips pens do not respond to different pressure, the colouring pencils are best to use for blended areas.

Class activities
- Children can develop their drawing until they are ready to add colour.
- Children can add colour to their work using the felt tips and colouring pencils.
- Encourage the children to look at the colour wheel and use complementary colours.

Plenary

Gather the children and ask them to pick out examples of their classmates' work that remind them of a composition that is like Rosenquist's. Ask the children to comment on work that has original ideas in it that work well, i.e. methods for joining images or ways of applying colour. Ask the children to look at their own work and think about what they would like to work on to complete the image next lesson.

Lesson 3 Pop art

Key artworks

James Rosenquist, *President Elect*, oil on Masonite™, 1960–61/1964
Preparatory collage for *President Elect*

You will need

- Key artworks on a slideshow and a handout
- Children's artwork from previous lesson, including their source collages
- A large collection of images and lettering taken from popular packaging, e.g. parts of cereal boxes or juice boxes (so the children can refer to these for additional ideas about how to merge their three main images)
- Pencils and erasers
- Good quality felt tips
- Colouring pencils
- Sticky notes

Preparation

Set the materials out on tables so that the children can easily select what they need.

Getting started

Encourage the children to look at their artwork so far and set themselves some targets for the lesson, they could do this on sticky notes so that can track their progress. They should look at their work and focus on how the main images have been merged and how the colour has been applied.

Class activities

- Children should continue to add colour to complete their image.
- Stop for peer or self-assessment as needed.

Plenary

Ask the children to present their work in small groups, talking about why they selected their images and how their work is like Rosenquist's work, including the colours used and the process of using the preparatory collage and scaling it up. Ask the children to discuss how it was to work with felt tips. Questions such as 'Why are they appropriate for this style of work?' and 'What are the limitations of using them?' can lead the discussion. Answers such as 'You cannot create tone with them' demonstrate good understanding.

Further activities

1. The children could use a computer, magazines and newspapers to select their own images for the source collages. This could be a homework task, enabling children to source images of their favourite celebrities/logos/adverts.
2. The children could use paints instead of the felt tips, allowing them the chance to use the paints to achieve a different effect, e.g. flat, bold colour.
3. If the children find the enlarging process challenging, you could have them trace over their source collage and then you could enlarge the tracing on a photocopier, ready for the next lesson.

Cross-curricular links

Computing: The children could use computer editing programmes to merge images – this will give the children more freedom to rotate, enlarge, reduce, flip, etc. The children could then use the computer-generated image to draw and paint from.

History: The children could use images of an important character from history and/or advertisements from that era, i.e. what would have been popular culture at that time.

8 Matisse: Collage

In 30 seconds...

In these lessons, the children will look at the collage work of Henri Matisse (1869–1954). They will understand how the artist made compositional choices based on balancing colour and shape, and they will create their own collages using the same Rembrandt masterpiece that Matisse used as inspiration.

Key artworks

Henri Matisse, *The Sorrows of the King*, gouache on paper on canvas, 1952
Rembrandt Harmenszoon van Rijn, *Saul and David*, oil on panel, 1630

What do I need to know?

Henri Matisse was a French artist and is widely regarded as an artist whose skilful use of colour could rival or at least match that of Picasso. Matisse's body of work is expansive and includes drawing, painting, murals, sculpture and in later life, collage or, *drawing with scissors* as he named it. Although Matisse explored many approaches stylistically, he was always concerned with the character of things and strove to produce art that had aesthetic balance. Aged seventy and around the time of the start of the Second World War, Matisse found himself living in an empty studio with bare walls. His wife and he had recently separated and many of his belongings were in storage. In addition to this, the artist was suffering frequently debilitating bouts of illness following a diagnosis of cancer. This challenging time of Matisse's life ended up being a period in which he produced some of his best-known and most uplifting and vibrant work.

In the past, Matisse had used paper cut-outs as a way of planning larger paintings, but this technique became an art form in itself – especially fitting when intestinal surgery meant he spent his time either in bed or a wheelchair. Eventually Matisse produced most of his work from his studio, which he referred to as his *Factory* in Nice, where assistants would paint gouache colours onto paper, mixing the colours to the artist's precise instructions. Matisse would then meticulously cut the painted paper into shapes, keeping and using both the shape and the remnants. The assistants would move and pin the shapes onto canvas or the walls of the studio, forming a large-scale collage, with every movement carefully directed by Matisse. Often a single artwork would remain in progress for months.

The Sorrows of the King is known to be Matisse's last self-portrait and is a piece that he made late in his life. The artist is represented by the black form and is surrounded by the things that bring him joy, such as music. The work pays homage to another painting, *Saul and David* by Rembrandt, in which the young David distracts the king from his melancholic state with music; the king is so moved that we see him wiping a tear from his eye. In *The Sorrows of the King* cut-out, Matisse is depicting old age and the tendency to reminisce on the pleasures in life, whilst also acknowledging the healing power of artistic beauty.

- During the early to mid 1940s, Matisse was in poor health and following surgery, he started using a wheelchair. By 1950, he stopped painting altogether in favour of his vibrantly coloured paper cut-outs.
- Matisse worked in a studio where he had his assistants paint white paper with gouache paint; he then **meticulously** cut shapes out of the coloured paper using scissors.
- Matisse would then instruct his assistants, who arranged and rearranged the cut-outs to find a **balanced composition**, before mounting the pieces on canvas or onto the studio walls.
- This work pays **homage** to one of Rembrandt's canvases, *Saul and David*.
- The artwork can be said to **symbolise** the power of music and the arts to heal, soothe and relax.

Vocabulary

Balanced composition: The arrangement of the formal elements of art in relation to each other.
Homage: Something done with respect to, or acknowledgement of another or another's work.
Meticulously: Showing extreme care and being precise.
Symbolise: Represent or stand for something.

Useful links

www.henrimatisse.org A website dedicated to life and work of the artist
www.artbible.info/art/large/378.html *Saul and David*
www.henrimatisse.org/sorrow-of-the-king.jsp *The Sorrow of the King*
youtu.be/GN0okOq8Hyc Video footage of Matisse creating and arranging cut out shapes

---

Lesson 1 Painting paper

Key artwork
Henri Matisse, *The Sorrows of the King*, gouache on paper on canvas, 1952

You will need
- White A3 paper, photocopy paper will work as their needs to be enough for each child to paint several colours onto (minimum of five sheets each or more)
- Poster paints
- Mixing palettes
- Large flat brushes
- Water pots
- Aprons

Preparation
Lay piles of the white paper out on the tables and ensure that there is drying space for the papers as they are painted, the children will be coating several sheets each. Fill the palettes with a selection of colours; you could limit the children to the primary colours to challenge them to mix their own colours. Make sure each child has access to the water pot and a brush.

Getting started

Show the children the key artwork and discuss what the possible story is in the work – you will discuss this in more detail during the plenary. Focus the children on working out which materials were used in the key artwork, prompt by asking them whether it is a painting or drawing and ask them to suggest how they can tell, i.e. can they see that the image is made from separate bits of paper? Tell the children about Matisse and explain how he came to use cut-outs instead of paint. Encourage the children to understand how Matisse must have been determined to continue to create and not to let his disability stop him from doing this. Talk about the technique of painting the paper first and then cutting shapes from it, rather than using images cut from magazines or coloured paper. Explain to the children that they will be using a similar technique to Matisse to create their own collage and that the first step will be to paint their sheets of paper so that they are dry for next lesson. Tell them that you are deliberately holding back on what colours are available as you want them to focus on mixing original colours rather than the ready-made colours – you could also share that the paper they create will be for everyone to use next lesson.

Class activities

- Remind the children how to mix secondary colours and how to make shades and tints of colours.
- Demonstrate how to use the flat brush repetitively in the same direction to get a smoother finish.
- Allow the children to mix their own colours and paint the white pieces of paper.
- The children should make their decisions based purely on creating interesting colours – they do not need to know what they will be creating with the coloured paper next lesson.
- The children do not need to name their work, as they will be sharing each other's paper next lesson.

Plenary

Gather the children and look at the key artwork again. Ask them if they can see anything recognisable in the collage such as figures, leaves, an instrument. Ask the children what they think the figures are doing, i.e. one is playing an instrument. Ask the children to discuss differences in the way that the artist has depicted the figures, i.e. one is playing an instrument and one is listening and has more decorative, wavy lines. Tell the children that next lesson they will be using the painted paper to make a collage.

Lesson 2 Meticulous cutting

Key artworks

Henri Matisse, *The Sorrows of the King*, gouache on paper on canvas, 1952
Rembrandt Harmenszoon van Rijn, *Saul and David*, oil on panel, 1630

You will need

- The painted paper from last lesson – now dry
- Scissors

- Blu-Tack™
- Copies of the Rembrandt key artwork, enough for the class
- A3 white paper or card for the children to stick their cut-outs to
- A4 envelopes or paperclips for storing loose cut out shapes in, one each

Preparation
Have all the materials within easy reach for the children and distribute a range of papers on each table. Each child should be able to see a copy of the Rembrandt image.

Getting started
Display the two key artworks side by side on the board and ask the children if they can see any similarities, discuss how Matisse was inspired by the Rembrandt painting. Ask the children how they think Matisse changed the Rembrandt to make it his own. Tell the children that although the collage may look much more simplistic, Matisse has considered where to place colours and shapes, and he would explore different compositions before committing to sticking the paper down. Ask the children to discuss what they think Matisse was looking for, i.e. when did he know it was time to stick? There is no right answer to this and the children can come up with their own criteria, remind them that as artists they can trust their own opinions on when something looks good.

Look at some examples of the colours that the children used last lesson and allow the children to comment on how the colours make them feel or what they remind them of. Ask the children if they can remember what the next step in Matisse's technique was, after painting the paper. Tell the children that the artist would then use his scissors to create the shapes he wanted. Explain that the children will be making their own version of the Rembrandt work that Matisse used as inspiration, but be sure to emphasise that it does not have to be a direct copy, they should merely use it as a stimulus for their own work. Tell the children that this lesson no one will stick with the glue, they will only temporarily tack cut-outs so that they can experiment with different compositions first.

Class activities
- Remind the children how to cut effectively – show them the video clip of Matisse cutting (youtu.be/GN0okOq8Hyc).
- Allow the children to cut shapes out of the coloured paper and tack them or just collect them in their envelopes ready for next lesson.

Plenary
Allow the children to share some of the shapes that they have cut and explain what inspired them, remembering that they did not have to directly copy the Rembrandt image. It could be that some of the children cannot explain their shapes because they were engrossed in the act of cutting and creating shapes – this is fine; you could encourage them to describe how that felt. Explain to the children that next lesson they will be arranging the shapes to make a 'final' composition.

Lesson 3 Directing a balanced composition

Key artworks
Henri Matisse, *The Sorrows of the King*, gouache on paper on canvas, 1952
Rembrandt Harmenszoon van Rijn, *Saul and David*, oil on panel, 1655–1650

You will need

- The painted paper from first lesson – now dry
- Shapes from last lesson in the children's envelopes
- Scissors
- Blu-Tack™
- Glue sticks
- A3 white paper or card, one each
- A4 envelopes or paperclips for storing cut out shapes in

Getting started
Look at the different shapes that the children have created and demonstrate how the children can now 'play' with their compositions, placing their cut-outs onto the A3 white paper or card. Encourage the children to think about how the colours and shapes look next to each other to try and create a balanced composition. Ask the children if they can recall how Matisse went about arranging his cut-out shapes, and remind them that because he was in a wheelchair, he asked his assistants to help him. Tell the children that today they will be instructing a partner to arrange their shapes and make their collage. Discuss with the children whether they think this will be challenging and emphasise that they must practise good listening and give clear instructions. Ensure that the children can use instructions effectively, e.g. rotate, top left or bottom centre. It could be helpful to demonstrate this process with a willing volunteer.

Class activities
- Split the remaining lesson time into two and have the children work in pairs to direct each other about where to stick the shapes – they can use the Blu-Tack™ before committing to their composition.
- Remind the children that they can use the Rembrandt painting as inspiration.
- Ensure that the children are allowing each other to do all the sticking for their artworks, no cheating!

Plenary
Gather the children and look at their artworks, discussing how the works link to the Rembrandt image, if at all. Ask the children to share how it felt not to be in total physical control of arranging their work. Discuss how it felt to be directed by the artist and not having any input even though you might have an opinion.

Further activities

1. Space permitting, you could have the children work on one large piece, tacking shapes to a wall space in the classroom. You could have a few assistants and the children could take turns directing them.

Cross-curricular links

Computing: The children could plan their collage first using the computer, manipulating shapes and exploring compositions.

Maths: The children could make a collage using shapes that they have learnt about.

9 Benin Empire: Cardboard relief sculpture

In 30 seconds...

In these lessons, the children will learn about the prosperous Benin Empire by looking at the pendant mask of the king's mother. The children will read and understand how the mask uses symbols to show the success of Benin and its rulers. The children will use cardboard and craft techniques to create their own relief mask inspired by the key artwork.

Key artwork

Benin ivory Queen Mother pendant mask: *Iyoba*, carved elephant ivory mask-shaped hip pendant, inlaid with iron and bronze, sixteenth century

---

What do I need to know?

The Benin Empire began in the west of Africa around 900 BC, in the area that is now Nigeria. What began as small settlements in clearings of the African rainforest would become a powerful empire by the 1400s. For 200 or so years, the Benin Empire was extremely successful. Its geographical position meant that the river Niger provided trade routes with other African kingdoms. The South Atlantic Ocean provided opportunities to trade goods with Europe, and starting with the Portuguese in the 1400s, Benin did this with great success. Traders and merchants would return from Benin to places all over Europe, telling stories of the impressive Benin Empire. Benin had an accomplished tradition of music, art and crafts, and the west has always been fascinated with the sculptures and relief work produced by Benin's skilled craft workers. The kingdom was ruled by a king, known as the *oba* in Yoruba (one of four official languages of Nigeria). There were at least 24 obas of the Benin Empire from 1440 to 1897.

The people believed that the oba was akin to a god, and he preserved this belief by remaining apart from the ordinary people, undertaking his leadership from the privacy of the royal palace and courts. The oba relied on many important people to help him rule the empire. Idia was the name of the mother of Oba Esigie who ruled from 1504 to 1547. Idia is known as the first 'queen mother' and she was so influential that Oba Esigie had a palace built just for her. The term *iyoba* means queen mother.

The end of the Benin Empire came in 1897 when the British met resistance from the then oba to agree terms of trade. Infuriated by this, the British invaded Benin and made it part of the British Empire. Over 4,000 artworks were taken from the Benin collection and some were even sold by the British to pay for the expedition.

The key artwork depicts Idia, the queen mother, and in fact it would not have been worn as a mask on the head but as a pendant around the waist of the oba during ceremonies. The small figures along the top of the mask depict the heads of Portuguese merchants; this represents the fact that Benin had strong trading relationships with Portugal whilst also symbolising the wider success of the empire. The Portuguese heads are interspersed with mudfish which symbolise the oba's position as both the divine leader living in the land of the gods and the king living on earth. Mudfish survive in two environments; they can live in both land and sea. The mask is made from elephant ivory which is one of the precious commodities that attracted foreign trade with Benin and has a colour associated with a god symbolising wealth.

- From the 1400s and up until its **invasion** by the British in 1897, Benin was a thriving **empire**.
- The king of Benin was known as the **oba** and he ruled both as a god and an earthy leader.
- The Benin empire was successful in **trading** with other African empires and Europe.
- The Portuguese **merchants** were the first to trade with Benin.
- The key artwork shows Idia, the oba's mother, and is in fact a **pendant** to be worn around the oba's waist.
- Idia helped Oba Esigie to rule his empire and was an important figure of the Benin royal court.
- The mask also shows Portuguese traders and mudfish; it is made from elephant ivory.

Vocabulary

Empire: A group of states or countries ruled over by a person or small group of people with supreme power.

Invasion: An entrance to overrun or take possession.

Merchant: A person involved with trade.

Oba: A hereditary ruler of the people of Benin.

Pendant: A piece of jewellery that hangs from a chain around the neck.

Relief: A type of sculpture in which the work projects from but is attached to a wall, or other type of background surface, on which it is carved.

Trading: Buying and selling goods or services.

Useful links

www.bbc.co.uk/guides/z3n7mp3 Information about Benin
www.britishmuseum.org/research/collection_online/collection_object_details.aspx?objectId=621190&partId=1 Iyoba pendant mask
www.britishmuseum.org/pdf/KingdomOfBenin_Presentation.pdf Photographs of the British expedition

Lesson 1 The Benin Empire

Key artwork
Benin ivory Queen Mother pendant mask: *Iyoba*, carved elephant ivory mask-shaped hip pendant, inlaid with iron and bronze, sixteenth century

You will need
- A3 (or larger) white or beige cartridge paper
- White chalk
- Charcoal
- Copies of the key artwork – class set
- Magnifying glasses – class set or one between two

Preparation
Print copies of the key artwork.

Getting started
Before showing the key artwork, ask the children if they can name any empires and explain to them they will be learning about the Benin Empire. Ask a child to locate Nigeria on a map and discuss whether any of the children have any links to Nigeria. Show the children the artwork, and explain that before you discuss and learn about the artwork, the children will be making a close observational study of it. Tell the children that through making a large copy of work, they will be looking really closely at it and may notice some clues as to what it is, when it was made, who or what it depicts, and what is made from. Tell them they will have the magnifying glasses to help with this.

Class activities
- Give the children copies of the key artwork as well as paper, chalk, charcoal and magnifying glasses.
- Ask the children to make a large copy of the mask with as much detail as possible – they should try to capture the textures and tones of the mask too.
- Use the fixative or hairspray to coat the children's work after they have gone, this will stop it from smudging.

Plenary
Ask the children to feedback what they discovered through making their reproductions. Ask the children if they have any ideas about the date of the piece and help them by telling them that around the same time, King Henry VIII was king of England. Allow the children to share who they think the mask could be depicting, encouraging them to think about who would be important enough to warrant this being made in their image. Reveal the information about the mask, including what the detail around the head represents and the material used. Give the children some background about the Benin Empire.

Lesson 2 Cardboard techniques

Key artwork
Benin ivory Queen Mother pendant mask: *Iyoba*, carved elephant ivory mask-shaped hip pendant, inlaid with iron and bronze, sixteenth century

You will need
- The children's drawings from the previous lesson
- Copy of the key artwork
- An A4 piece of card for each child, the children will build their relief on this
- Scraps of card in varying sizes, textures and thickness
- Scissors
- PVA glue
- Glue spreaders
- Pencils

Preparation
It would be useful to prepare your own cardboard relief mask, with one half developed to a finished state and the other in progress – you can then use this to demonstrate with. Lay all the materials out so that the children can easily reach them.

Getting started
Ask the children to share what they can remember about the key artwork and the Benin Empire. Remind them that although the piece looks like a mask, it was in fact a pendant. Explain that they will be making their own version of the pendant using cardboard relief. This could also be a good time to talk with the children about ivory and why it is now an illegal trade. Tell the children that they will be using the printouts of the key artwork and their observational studies to create a piece of relief work. Explain to the children that although a relief has 3D elements like a sculpture, a sculpture can be viewed from all angles, whereas a relief is usually only visible from the front. Demonstrate to the children how they can translate the two-dimensional shapes from the print out of the image and their drawing into relief shapes by building up different layers with the cardboard. Show the children how they can use their pencils to incise patterns onto the cardboard and that they can peel away layers of the cardboard to reveal different textures. Encourage the children to attach and join, to incise and to create relief work on their mask.

Class activities
- Give the children copies of the key artwork as well as their own drawings from the previous lesson.
- Allow the children to sketch out the basic design onto the main piece of A4 cardboard.
- Children can select, layer, cut and incise the cardboard to reproduce the pendant of Idia.
- Allow the children to embellish and adapt the design if they want to.

Plenary
Gather the children and their work to look at strong examples of different techniques being used in the class. Ask the children to share tips about how they accomplished effects with the cardboard.

Lesson 3 Idia in cardboard relief

Key artwork
Benin ivory Queen Mother pendant mask: *Iyoba*, carved elephant ivory mask-shaped hip pendant, inlaid with iron and bronze, sixteenth century

You will need
* The children's cardboard work from the previous lesson
* The children's drawings from the previous lesson
* Copy of the key artwork
* An A4 piece of card for each child
* Scraps of card in varying sizes, textures and thickness
* Scissors
* PVA glue
* Glue spreaders
* Pencils
* Sticky notes

Getting started
Ask the children to remind each other of some of the techniques they have been using to layer, incise and embellish the cardboard. Ask the children to look at their own work and write three targets for today's lesson, relating to the inclusion of different techniques. The children could write their targets onto sticky notes, e.g. use multiple layers or use a wider variety of shapes.

Class activities
* Allow the children to use their targets and continue with their relief sculptures.

Plenary
Gather the children and look at the key artwork. Ask the children to select the relief sculptures that they think look most impressive and to explain why. Ask the children to imagine that their work is going to be inspected by the oba and his mother; ask them to think about the how the craftspeople of Benin might have felt when creating art for the oba.

Further activities

1. The children could make their relief work using clay or modelling clay instead of cardboard.
2. The children could make masks using their own or their classmates' faces as inspiration, pretending that they have been commissioned to make the portrait look as regal and important as possible. They could decorate their mask with symbols of things that are important to the sitter, e.g. musical instruments or sports equipment.

Cross-curricular links

History: You could teach this alongside a scheme about Henry VIII and compare the depictions of rulers from different continents at similar times. Holbein's *Portrait of Henry VIII* is a good painting to use for comparison.

History: This scheme could form part of a wider history scheme where the children learn about the Benin Empire.

Geography: This scheme could run alongside a topic about trade routes.

10 Impressionism: Painting en plein air

In 30 seconds...

In these lessons, the children will learn about the Impressionist movement and what set the paintings apart from other art being produced in Europe at that time. They will look at the key artwork by Monet (1840–1926), which provoked the name 'Impressionists'. They will learn how to mix shades and tints and will experience painting 'en plein air' using the quick brush strokes of the Impressionist artists.

Key artworks

Claude Monet, *Impression, Sunrise*, oil on canvas, 1872
Claude Monet, *The Port of Le Havre, Night Effect*, oil on canvas, 1873
Claude Monet, *The Grand Dock at Le Havre*, oil on canvas, 1872

What do I need to know?

The movement known as Impressionism began in France in about 1860 and was instigated by a group of artists, many still well-known today, who rejected the status quo of art at the time. This group of artists included Pissarro, Renoir, Degas, and Monet, to name a few, and they initially called themselves *The Anonymous Society of Painters, Sculptors and Printmakers*. The artists' styles and subject matters varied, but what unified them was that they had all, at different times, been rejected by *the Salon*. At that time in France, the only way to show your work to the public and reach notability in the art world was to exhibit at the Salon's annual exhibition, and the Salon had a tough academic jury that were responsible for deciding whose work would make it. Not wanting to wait for yearly intervals to have a chance of exhibiting, this group of artists did something unprecedented at that time – they organised their own exhibitions. The first was in 1874, and they held several subsequent exhibitions over the next decade or so.

These artists revolutionised painting. Much of the well-respected art at the time was made to fit into established categories such as portraiture, genre paintings, and historical or religious stories. The Impressionists did not want to be limited to these subject matters, they wanted freedom of choice and often painted 'ordinary' people and scenes; this was considered inappropriate at the time. The Impressionists tried to capture fleeting moments in time by recording the subtleties of changing light and movement; they often did this using loose, short, fast brushstrokes, which also went against the painting traditions of the day. These artists were often accused of creating paintings that looked unfinished due to the non-traditional way that they applied paint to the canvas, often brush marks remained visible with tints and shades of colour layered or placed near to each other, rather than blended neatly. Another radical move for this group of painters was that they often took to painting outdoors or *en plein air*, as they recognised that the production of portable, tubed oil paints and the box easel meant that artists no longer had to work from a studio. By working outdoors, the Impressionists could paint directly from life and they would work fast to capture changes as they occurred, e.g. in atmosphere, water surfaces and expressions.

The exhibition in 1874 was where Monet first showed his work *Impression, Sunrise*, and it is at this point that the Impressionists became known as such. The famous art critic of the time, Louis Leroy, said that Monet's painting looked like an unfinished sketch or an 'impression' – he meant this as an insult. The artist made several paintings of the same harbour in Le Havre, at different times of day and from different angles, an approach common to the Impressionists and also seen in Monet's famous waterlilies series.

- The Impressionists **revolutionised** painting with the style we now know as **Impressionism**.
- They were rejected by the **Salon** as their work was not seen as suitable or in keeping with the art traditions of the time.
- They organised their own exhibition, rebuffing the Salon as the only means for exhibiting in France at that time.
- The Impressionists painted **en plein air** and used tubed paints and a **box easel** that had recently become available.
- They tried to capture changes in light by using fast, loose **brushstrokes**.
- The Impressionists left brush marks on the canvas, with **shades** and **tints** visible and unblended.
- The Impressionists got the collective name when a critic insulted Monet's work saying that is looked like an '**impression**'.

Vocabulary

Box easel: A freestanding easel that includes a compartment to store paints and brushes, etc. Some also include a handle or straps so they can be carried like a backpack or suitcase.
Brushstroke: The mark made by a paintbrush.
En plein air: A French phrase meaning 'open (in full) air', and refers to the way that Impressionist artists painted outdoors.
Exhibition: A public display of work or art.
Impression: An idea, feeling or opinion about something or someone, often formed on first contact.
Impressionism: A style of painting developed in the last third of the nineteenth century.
Revolutionised: To change something radically.
Salon: In nineteenth-century France, the Salon was the official annual art exhibition in France; it was where all the esteemed artists would exhibit their work, and where important figures in French society would gather to discuss art and culture.
Shade: A darker version of an original colour made by adding black.
Tint: A lighter version of an original colour made by adding white.

Useful links

www.khanacademy.org/humanities/becoming-modern/avant-garde-france/impressionism/ a/a-beginners-guide-to-impressionism A guide to Impressionism

www.nationalgallery.org.uk/paintings/learn-about-art/guide-to-impressionism/guide-to-impressionism A guide to Impressionism
www.totallyhistory.com/impression-sunrise *Impression, sunrise*
www.wikiart.org/en/claude-monet/the-port-of-le-havre-night-effect *The Port Of Le Havre*
www.wikiart.org/en/claude-monet/the-grand-dock-at-le-havre-1872 *The Grand Dock at Havre*
youtu.be/BJE4QUNgaeg Monet painting in in his garden

Lesson 1 Painting skills

Key artwork
Claude Monet, *Impression, Sunrise*, oil on canvas, 1872

You will need

- Poster paints – primary colours, black and white
- Palettes
- Wide, flat head brushes
- Water pots
- A3 paper
- Tissues for dabbing brushes
- Aprons

Preparation
Ensure that all the children have access to
water pots, brushes and a palette with three primary colours and black and white.

Getting started
Show the children the key artwork and ask them to share their first impressions of it. Ask them to comment on the brush marks, colours and light. Explain to the children that they will be learning about the Impressionists and discuss who they were and why they were so important and revolutionary. Explain that just because these artists bucked the trend, it did not mean that they were not skilled artists. Tell the children that they will be practising some of the techniques used by artists including the Impressionists. Explain that the children will be learning how to make shades and tints of colours as well as how to make different marks with the brushes, which will enable them to make better paintings in the future.

Class activities
- Give the children an A3 piece of paper, a brush, access to a water pot and a palette with the three primary colours and black and white in it.
- Explain to the children that they will select a colour and try to make as many different marks with it on the paper as possible, e.g. dashes in varying lengths, dots, thin lines, thick lines, smudge marks. The children could look at the key artwork for ideas about brush marks.
- Next, ask the children to select another colour and make a series of six thick dashes with it.
- Let the children add a small amount of white to one of the dashes and then increase the amount of white to make different tints of the original colour.
- Do the same with black – the children should find that white makes the original colour

lighter – known as a 'tint'. They should also find that black makes the original colour darker – known as a 'shade'.

Plenary
Gather the children and discuss their findings. Ask them to feedback how they think the Impressionists might have used these skills to be able to work quickly to record their chosen view. Explain that the Impressionists would have been using oil paints, which are very slow to dry. Tell the children that as well as mixing colours in palettes, sometimes artists mix the colours onto the canvas directly.

Lesson 2 En plein air

Key artwork
Claude Monet, *Impression, Sunrise*, oil on canvas, 1872

You will need
- Tins of watercolour paints
- Wide, flat head brushes and thin brushes
- Water pots – portable
- A4 paper on clipboards
- Tissues for dabbing brushes
- Aprons

Preparation
Decide where you will take the children to paint, e.g. a local park or the playground – you will need to return next lesson. It is really useful to put the paper onto the clipboards while in the classroom to save time when outside.

Getting started
Look at the video of Monet painting outside (youtu.be/BJE4QUNgaeg), and ask the children if they know the French term for this. Tell them it is *en plein air* and explain that it is a French term we use when talking about the Impressionists. Remind the children that the Impressionists used the newly-invented tubed paints and box easel in order to paint outdoors. Ask the children to give feedback about why the Impressionists found that working outside was more conducive to their style, e.g. they could capture changes immediately and as they were happening. Tell the children that they will be working en plein air this lesson, and ask them to share any challenges they think this will pose, e.g. light might change, wind might blow things, too cold or too hot, carrying materials. Tell the children that these are the same challenges that the Impressionists would have met and remind them that they will have to work fast.

Class activities
- Give the children their paper on a clipboard, the two types of brushes, a water pot to share and some tissue for dabbing.

- Remind the children of the techniques that they practised last lesson and remind them to use tints, shades and a range of brushstrokes.
- Be sure they know that they will be selecting which area of the location to paint – painting directly without sketching in pencil first as they might be used to.
- Take the children outside and allow them to choose an area of interest to paint. If there are interesting clouds and wind, they could even focus on the sky. Preferably the children would not choose a static object such as a section of a building.

Plenary
Bring the children back inside and discuss with them how it felt to work en plein air. Look at the paintings and highlight work that shows the artist has used a range of brushstrokes and mixed tints and shades well.

Lesson 3 Painting a series

Key artworks
Claude Monet, *Impression, Sunrise*, oil on canvas, 1872
Claude Monet, *The Port of Le Havre, Night Effect*, oil on canvas, 1873
Claude Monet, *The Grand Dock at Le Havre*, oil on canvas, 1872

You will need
- Tins of watercolour paints
- Wide, flat head brushes and thin brushes
- Water pots – portable
- A4 paper on clipboards
- Tissues for dabbing brushes
- Aprons

Preparation
Ensure that you can take the children back to the same location as last lesson.

Getting started
Look at the key artwork from last lesson, *Impressions, Sunrise*, and explain that it shows a sunset in Le Havre which was Monet's hometown and that Monet made several paintings of the harbour there. Explain that Monet made his paintings at different times of day and from different angles. Show the children the other two key artworks: *The Port of Le Havre, Night Effect*, and *The Grand Dock at Le Havre*. Explain that the children will be returning to the initial location and that they will need to paint the same view as last lesson but, where possible, from a different angle.

Class activities
- Give the children their paper on a clipboard, the two types of brushes, a water pot to share and some tissue for dabbing.

- Remind the children of the techniques that they practised last lesson and remind them to use tints, shades and a range of brushstrokes.
- Be sure they know that they will be painting directly without sketching in pencil first as they might be used to.
- Take the children outside and ask them to return to the same view from last lesson but ask them to view it from a different angle. If there are interesting clouds and wind, they could even focus on the sky more than the view.

Plenary
Bring the children back inside and discuss with them how it felt to work en plein air and with the same subject. Compare their two paintings, and discuss how they are similar and different.

Further activities

1. To emphasise the fact that the Impressionists tried to capture movement, the project could be done looking at the work of Edgar Degas, and the children could draw or paint PE lessons.

Cross-curricular links

Science: Children could experiment with different ways of making paints, using pigments from natural sources and binding with egg white. This demonstrates how much easier it would have been for artists to paint when tube paints became accessible.

11 Hokusai: Printing famous landmarks

In 30 seconds...

In these lessons, the children will look at the infamous woodblock print by the Japanese artist, Katsushika Hokusai (1760–1849). They will understand that the work is part of a series of prints which all depict Mount Fuji. The children will use images of well-known landmarks in their area and create lino prints of them.

Key artwork

Katsushika Hokusai, *The Great Wave Off Kanagawa*, woodblock print, 1830–1833 (see Figure 11A)

What do I need to know?

Katsushika Hokusai was a Japanese painter and printmaker. He worked during a period of artistic and cultural development in Japan, known as the Edo period. At this time, the country was experiencing long-awaited peace under the Tokugawa family, following years of civil turbulence. Not much is known about Hokusai's early life, but it is thought that his father was a mirror maker for the Tokugawa family and we do know that Hokusai changed his name several times throughout his career, to coincide with changes in his artistic style. Hokusai was the first Japanese artist to reach international fame, but this did not happen until after his death in 1849. Up until that point, Japan was a very isolated country. Hokusai's rise to fame was boosted in 1867, when the world's fair was held in France and it included a Japanese pavilion for the first time. Monet was among the visitors to the pavilion and he purchased several Japanese prints, a number of which were by Hokusai. Monet had these Japanese prints on display at his home in Giverny, where he also had a Japanese garden built and made a series of paintings that depicted it and the water lilies surrounding it. Hokusai's work was enjoyed by many other well-known artists such as Vincent van Gogh and Edgas Degas, and some say that his work influenced the Impressionist movement. Hokusai's most popular work was and is *Thirty-six Views of Mount Fuji*, which was created between 1826 and 1833, and the most renowned piece in this series is undoubtedly *The Great Wave off Kanagawa*, which has debatably become the most globally recognisable Japanese artwork.

Hokusai was passionate about Mount Fuji and he was part of a Buddhist group who believed that the mountain was associated with eternal life. In his series, *Thirty-Six views of Mount Fuji*, Hokusai shows the landmark in different weather conditions and from different angles, much like the Impressionists did later on. The Mount Fuji series was so well-received that Hokusai added a further ten prints to the series.

The prints were made using a woodblock printing technique that originated in China but was adopted by Japanese artists during the Edo period. The technique involves designs being drawn onto paper before being cut out of a woodblock, which was usually cherry wood. The woodblock is then covered in ink and applied to paper. This printing technique was frequently used to mass-produce images in Japan, and the prints were frequently sold as souvenirs. These prints were sold relatively cheaply, and many of the elite in the country were displeased at the popularity of the woodblock work as opposed to other Japanese arts and crafts.

The key artwork depicts Japanese cargo boats that were used to transport live fish from villages to Edo (modern day Tokyo). There are fishermen cowering in the face of the huge wave, although it could be said that they are following a well-practised routine in order to stay safe. In the hollow of the wave is Mount Fuji, it is snow-capped and appears small because of Hokusai's use of perspective. There is some debate over whether the wave is a tsunami; some experts say that the way the wave is breaking in the sea rather than on the shore means that it is more likely to be what is known as an abnormal wave. The crest of the wave is formed into tips that almost look like claws grasping down towards the fishermen, and the spray of the wave appears almost snow-like falling over the mountain.

- Katsushika Hokusai was a Japanese painter and **printmaker**.
- Hokusai worked during the **Edo period** in Japan.
- It is said that Hokusai influenced many western artists and many of them collected prints by the artist.
- Hokusai made a series of **woodblock prints** which all depict the Japanese **landmark**, Mount Fuji.
- Art critics and experts are uncertain about whether the great wave shows a **tsunami** or merely an abnormal wave.
- The prints were low-cost souvenirs and were not necessarily considered **high art** in Japan.
- The value of an **original print** only became an issue in the eighteenth and nineteenth centuries when artists started to sign their originals.

Vocabulary

Edo period: A period of great significance in Japan's history; the country was unified under the Tokugawa family after years of civil unrest.
High art: A concept used by societies to describe art that is created by a culturally-renowned and accepted artist.
Landmark: A feature of a landscape or town that is easily seen and recognised.
Original print: A print that is made directly from the artists' own woodblock or printing plate and printed by the artist.
Printmaker: An artist who makes pictures or designs by printing them from plates or blocks.
Tsunami: A high sea wave caused by an earthquake or other disturbance.
Woodblock print: A technique for printing text, images or patterns used extensively throughout East Asia and originating in China.

Useful links

www.khanacademy.org/humanities/art-asia/art-japan/edo-period/a/hokusai-under-the-wave-off-kanagawa-the-great-wave Information about the artist and his work
www.britishmuseum.org/whats_on/exhibitions/hokusais_great_wave.aspx *The Great Wave*

Lesson 1 Line drawing

Key artwork
Katsushika Hokusai, *The Great Wave Off Kanagawa*, woodblock print, 1830–1833

You will need
- Pencils
- Erasers
- Photos of landmarks from your local or surrounding area
- A4 paper
- Foam or polystyrene tiles for printing with

Preparation
Find or take and print images of your local area, focusing on landmarks that the children will recognise. Make a simple line drawing of one of the photographic images you have found of a landmark from your local or surrounding area. The drawing should be simple but include lines that vary in weight and length. The more variation you have, the more interesting the print will be (see Figure 11B and 11C for children's work).

Getting started
Look at the key artwork and ask the children to give feedback regarding what they can see in the image. Discuss the visual clues in the print and ask the children if they can guess what the landmark in the background is; use a map to track where the image is set. Explain to the children that this artwork is not a painting and ask them to suggest how the artist made it. Explain what is meant by a woodblock print and tell them that they will be making their own form of print but using slightly different materials, i.e. not wood. Show the children the images that you have collected which depict landmarks from the local or surrounding areas and show them how you took one of those images and simplified it to make a line drawing with no shading.

Class activities
- Allow the children to select one of the images as a resource to make a line drawing from. They could embellish or combine two or more images to design a more creative interesting composition.
- Ensure that the children keep in mind that the design should include lines, and tell them that this is important for the printing stage.
- The lines in the drawing can vary in weight and style to create more interest.

Plenary
Gather the children with their work and look at the line drawings, commenting on good compositions and what makes them so. Show the children the foam or polystyrene tile and demonstrate how they will need to transfer their line drawing onto the tile. Explain that to make sure that the tile doesn't rip or puncture, they will need to go over the lines gradually, building up layers of the drawing slowly rather than drawing with heavy lines first time around.

Lesson 2 Making the printing tile

Key artwork
Katsushika Hokusai, *The Great Wave Off Kanagawa*, woodblock print, 1830–1833

You will need
- Children's drawings from the previous lesson
- Pencils
- Foam or polystyrene tiles for printing with
- Rollers for printing
- Flat surface or tray palette for rolling ink onto
- Paper that is larger than your tile to print onto
- Newspaper
- Aprons

Preparation
Transfer your line drawing example from the previous lesson onto your foam or polystyrene tile.

Getting started
Recap the key artwork with the children and remind them that they are preparing to print images of landmarks from their own locality, inspired by Hokusai and Mount Fuji. Explain that the next stage is to transfer the line drawing onto what is called a 'printing tile', i.e. the foam or polystyrene tile. Remind the children that this needs to be built up gradually to avoid ripping the tile. You could demonstrate how easy it is to pierce the tile if you are too rough or heavy-handed.

Class activities
- Give the children their printing tile and allow them to transfer their image over to the tile.
- Make sure the children don't apply too much pressure to the tile; it may be helpful to supply some children with a scrap of tile to practise on first.

Plenary
Gather the children and look at their printing tiles. Ask the children to give feedback about how they found the process and any tips or challenges they would like to share. Using your example, demonstrate to the children how to roll the ink out onto the tray or the surface, listening out for the sticky sound that the ink makes when it is ready to print with. Next, place your printing tile onto the newspaper and roll ink over it, ensuring even coverage but not too much ink. When the print tile is ready, place the paper on top and rub all over the paper with your fingertips, making sure to reach all the parts of the tile underneath. Peel back the paper to reveal the print (see Figure 11C).

Lesson 3 Printing

Key artwork
Katsushika Hokusai, *The Great Wave Off Kanagawa*, woodblock print, 1830–1833

You will need
- Children's printing tiles from the previous lesson
- Printing ink
- Rollers for printing
- Newspaper
- Paper – enough for children to make multiple prints
- Aprons

Preparation
Lay newspaper out on the tables and place a tray palette with a small circle of printing ink at the top of each palette (or any flat surface that you are inking onto). Have piles of paper for printing onto somewhere that is easy to access for the children. You will also need somewhere that the children can take their wet prints to, keeping in mind that they will be making multiple prints each. This could work well with printing stations or children working in pairs to support each other.

Getting started
Recap the printing process with the class and explain the routines that you would like the children to follow, e.g. queuing up at the printing stations, or how to share equipment with their partners. Make sure that the children prepare by writing their names on the pieces of paper that they intend to print onto.

Class activities
- Allow the children to make as make as many prints as time permits.

Plenary
Ask the children to select their best print to show, and gather the children to look at their prints. Discuss with the children what makes some prints more successful than others, e.g. more or less ink, deeper lines on the printing tile, a fuller composition.

Further activities

1. The children could experiment with using different colours and different coloured paper. They could also refine their printing tile after the first few prints, making lines more defined and adding areas of interest to the print tile.

Cross-curricular links

Geography: The children could make prints of a landmark which links to a geography topic.
English: The children could make a print as an illustration to a story.

12 Robert Sweeney: Paper sculptures

In 30 seconds...

In these lessons, the children will look examples of paper sculptures and learn how this everyday medium can be used to create unique and intricate sculptures. The children will learn different paper construction, folding and joining techniques and will put them to use making a sculpture of their own.

Key artwork

Richard Sweeney, *O3M (Shell)*, watercolour paper, 2010 (see Figure 12A, and 12B and 12C for children's work)

What do I need to know?

The origins of paper art are connected to the history of paper, although it is not known how closely the two are linked in terms of dates. It can be assumed that sometime after the invention of paper, people began to experiment with manipulating it. Although papyrus and amate are types of ancient paper made from plants, the first type of wood pulp paper that we know today was invented in China in around the sixth century. The history of paper as used for recreational or artistic purposes is difficult to track, and there is some debate about it; some experts attest to evidence of paper folding as far back as ancient Egyptian times. The *Turin Papyrus map* is thought to be the first evidence of folded paper but the intention of the folds is unknown. What is known is that at some time after the production of paper, art forms such paper folding, or as it is commonly known, *origami* developed in East Asia, probably for ceremonial purposes. The word 'origami' is made up of two Japanese words: 'ori' meaning to fold and 'kami' meaning paper, and it refers to the Japanese form of paper folding art. The word *zhezhi* refers to the Chinese form. Although paper folding seems to originate in East Asia around the sixth century, there is some debate over whether it began in China or Japan, although there is little doubt that Japan fully developed and popularised the art form. That said, there is also a history of paper folding in Europe and although it begins later, some experts believe that this developed separately from the Eastern Asian paper crafts. There are references to paper folding in Spanish literature from the eighteenth century and, in sixteenth century England, the art of napkin folding used some of the same skills that are regarded as part of origami.

Paper cutting is another art form which appears to have originated in East Asia, but developed uniquely around the world. A good example of this is what is known as *papel picado*, which is a traditional Mexican form of paper cutting for decorative banners.

Traditional origami has ethics around using glue, size of paper, decoration of paper and how many sheets of paper to use. However, today there are many artists who have extended this art form and they use paper as a medium to cut, fold, bend, shape and construct with to make sculptures of great beauty. The work of Richard Sweeney (born 1984) is a good example of how this simple medium can produce impressive three-dimensional artworks.

- **Papyrus** and **amate** are ancient forms of paper.
- The first paper made from wood pulp has its **origins** in China.
- The use of paper folding as an art form began in **East Asia**.
- Japanese paper folding is known as **origami**, and Japan was the country to develop this art.
- Paper sculptures usually require the artist to have skills to **manipulate** and **construct** with the paper.

Vocabulary

Amate: Bark paper used by Mayans and Aztecs.
Construct: To build something.
Manipulate: Control in a skilful manner.
Origami: Japanese art of paper folding; the word is derived from two Japanese words: 'ori' meaning to fold and 'kami' meaning paper.
Origins: Where something begins, or is derived; its birthplace.
Papyrus: An ancient Egyptian paper made from the pith of a river plant.

Useful links

www.richardsweeney.co.uk/works Richard Sweeney's website
www.webdesignerdepot.com/2009/05/100-extraordinary-examples-of-paper-art Examples of paper art
www.paperonline.org/history-of-paper History of paper

Lesson 1 Paper sculpture skills

Key artwork
Richard Sweeney, *O3M (Shell)*, watercolour paper, 2010

You will need
- Strips of white paper (approximately 2.5cm width and 30cm length) enough for several per child
- Square pieces of white paper, enough for several per child

Preparation
Experiment with paper folding, bending, twisting, and cutting techniques, and stick these onto a piece of cardboard so that you can use this to show the children. (See Figure 12B and 12C for children's work.)

Getting started
Ask the children to tell you what they know about sculptures and the materials used for making them. Ask them to think of any alternative materials that artists might use. Share the work of Richard Sweeney and discuss paper art in relation to origami and the East. Explain to the children that they will be making their own paper sculptures, but first they need to learn some construction and manipulation skills. Show the children your examples and ask them if they can work out how some of them were made. Demonstrate how to use folding, twisting and rolling to make forms with the paper.

Class activities
- Allow the children some time to experiment or 'play' with the experiment and see what forms they can create.
- Encourage the children to share techniques with each other, demonstrating how to make forms as they work.

Plenary
Gather the children with their paper creations and ask them to share techniques that they developed. Encourage the children to describe their method to each other using step-by-step instructions.

Lesson 2 Constructing, manipulating and sticking

Key artwork
Richard Sweeney, *O3M (Shell)*, watercolour paper, 2010

You will need
- Strips of white paper (approximately 2.5cm width and 30cm length) enough for several per child
- Square pieces of white paper, enough for several per child
- A4 board or cardboard in black, one per child

Preparation

Creatively stick your strips of paper onto a piece of A4 cardboard by folding, bending and twisting them, creating a whole piece made of the smaller pieces. Think about how you want the separate parts to relate to each other (see Figure 12B and 12C for children's work).

Getting started

Ask some of the children to demonstrate different paper sculpting techniques. Encourage the children to also share any challenges that they had last lesson and see if the class can help. Explain that this lesson the children will be making one paper sculpture on an A4 board. Describe how the children will need to consider where they stick the individual paper sculptures to make one whole three-dimensional piece.

Class activities

- Let the children create their sculptures and stick them onto their board.
- Tell the children that because they are creating a sculpture it will be viewed from all angles, so the children need to turn the work as they create it.

Plenary

Gather the children with their paper sculptures and ask them to share techniques that they developed. Encourage the children to describe their methods to each other using step-by-step instructions.

Lesson 3 Three-dimensional paper sculpture

Key artwork

Richard Sweeney, O3M (Shell), watercolour paper, 2010

You will need

- Strips of white paper (approximately 2.5cm width and 30cm length), enough for several per child
- Corn paper
- Square pieces of white paper, enough for several per child
- Children's work from last lesson

Preparation

Add to your sculpture by including corn paper that has been folded to create shadows.

Getting started

Look at the children's sculptures so far and encourage them to view their work from all angles and to think about the composition. Encourage the children to share any challenges that they are experiencing and see if the class can help by doing practical demonstrations for each other. Ask the children to look again at the key artwork and ask them to notice how the shadows form an additional element to the work, ask the children to try and use the shadows in their work as part of their design.

Class activities

- Let the children continue to work on their sculptures.

Plenary

Gather the children with their paper creations and ask them to comment on each other's work, bringing to attention work in which the children have used a range of paper construction and manipulation techniques and which have interesting shadows. Ask the children if there were any challenges to working with this material. This would be a good time to show the children some other examples of paper art (see *Useful links*, page 105).

Further activities

1. The children could experiment with making freestanding paper sculptures instead of using the board as a base. They could also try working in groups with A1 paper to make large-scale sculptures.

Cross-curricular links

Design and technology: This project could be used as a design project by asking the children to design a building or play area using these techniques.

13 Pompeii: Mosaic

In 30 seconds...

In these lessons, the children will look at the sea creature mosaic found in ruins of Pompeii. They will draw and paint their own studies of sea creatures, then cut and reassemble them to make a mosaic out of paper.

Key artwork

Pompeii, *Sea Creature Mosaic*, first century AD

What do I need to know?

Believed to have been built in the second century BC, the decorative *House of the Faun* in Pompeii offers a good example of aristocratic life and taste in the Roman republic era. Within the house, archaeologists discovered elaborate decorations and mosaics that were preserved in the aftermath of the eruption of Mount Vesuvius, which occurred in AD 79. Although many artefacts and artworks were discovered, the most impactful of the findings were the remains of the human inhabitants that had been frozen in time.

Perhaps the most famous of the artworks found in the House of the Faun was the *Alexandra Mosaic*, depicting a moment of retreat from a battle scene between Alexandra the Great and Darius III in 333 BC. The sea creature mosaic is less historically informative but perhaps more immediately entertaining and accessible for all. The mosaic comprehensively captures a variety of marine food available at the time, most of which can still be found in that area today. The mosaic would have formed part of a central panel on the floor and was possibly a menu of sorts for the House of the Faun residents and its visitors. The composition includes a variety of sea creatures such as squid and eel; the centre of the composition shows an octopus wrapping its tentacles around a crayfish; there is even a small bird on a rock towards the left side of the composition. Although the image is made of tiles or tesserae, it includes an impressive amount of detail and even depicts shades and tints of colours that reflect the true nature of the sea creatures.

Mosaics are images made up of an assemblage of small pieces of marble, ceramics, glass or other materials. Most are made of small square-shaped tiles known as tesserae. Some of the earliest forms of mosaics were made of river pebbles and found in Ancient Greece. Later the Romans continued to use mosaics as a popular form of floor, ceiling and wall decoration. During the Renaissance period, the technique experienced a decline and was often replaced with fresco painting, which allowed for more intricate details. However, the tradition of mosaic is still alive today and artists and craftspeople use a variety of materials and create them in a range of settings, frequently in public spaces such as parks.

The tesserae can be placed in different formations of rows and columns, in a similar way to how an artist can utilise different brushstrokes. The visual flow of tesserae, known as the 'andamento', has an impact on the overall look of the mosaic and some approaches are easier to execute than others. The different styles of andamento relate to how the tesserae are laid out: a regular grid pattern is known as 'opus regulatum'; a design where the tesserae vary in size and shape and are placed haphazardly is known as 'opus palladianum'.

- The House of the Faun was one of the largest and most decorative houses in **Pompeii**.
- The House of the Faun provides an insight into the lives and interests of the **aristocrats** living in Rome at that time.
- The house contained many artefacts and artworks, including **mosaics** such as the Alexandra Mosaic and the sea creature mosaic.
- The sea creature mosaic is thought to have been a menu, showing the variety of **marine** creatures available at the time.
- The mosaic shows some details of the creatures and shows a range of shades and tints, which help to make the image more realistic.
- Mosaics can be created using different techniques related to the formation of the **tesserae**.
- The visual flow of the tesserae is known as the **andamento**.
- Mosaics come in different styles, such as **opus regulatum** and **opus palladianum**.

Vocabulary

Andamento: The visual flow of a mosaic.
Aristocrats: A privileged class of people, through education, rank or social prestige.
Marine: Found in the sea.
Mosaic: A piece of art made by assembling small pieces of glass, ceramics or other materials.
Opus palladianum: A design where the tesserae vary in size and shape and are placed haphazardly.
Opus regulatum: A design where the tesserae form a regular grid pattern.
Pompeii: An ancient city in Italy that was buried and preserved by the eruption of Mount Vesuvius.
Tesserae: Small pieces of a material used to make a mosaic.

Useful links

www.alexandermosaik.de/en The Alexander mosaic
www.britishmuseum.org/whats_on/exhibitions/pompeii_and_herculaneum/pompeii_live/ eruption_timeline.aspx The Pompeii mosaic

Lesson 1 Opus regulatum

Key artwork

Anonymous, *Sea Creature Mosaic*, first century AD

You will need

- A4 images of sea creatures
- A4 paper with a grid inserted onto it, one for each child. (see **Bloomsbury Online Resource 13A**)
- Pencils
- Erasers

Preparation

Find and print a selection of images of A4 sea creatures; these should be large clear images without too many intricate details or background images, i.e. simple enough for the children to reproduce. It is a good idea to source at least three or four images to cater for different abilities. See **Bloomsbury Online Resource 13A**, or use a word processor to create a grid on an A4 sheet yourself. Do this by going to 'insert table' and selecting the number of columns and rows – the fewer squares, the simpler the mosaic will be to create, i.e. it will be easier to cut out fewer squares and reassemble them into the mosaic. Keep in mind that the grid needs to fit the proportions of an A4 page so there should be more rows than columns (a good guide is a table of 4x3 as a minimum).

You should make your own drawing of one of the sea creatures onto the gridded paper, showing how to keep to scale, fill the page and include shapes and lines that you see.

Getting started

Look at the key artwork and ask the children to share what they see, ask them if they can see what it is made from, i.e. is it a painting or a drawing? Is it on paper? Explain to the children where the image is from and give them some information about Pompeii. Ask the children to share any ideas about why these sea creatures might have been used to decorate a house in Pompeii. Explain to the children about the mosaic method and how the tiles are known as tesserae. Tell the children that they will be making a simple form of mosaic and show them the pre-printed grid that will help them, tell the children that their final mosaic will be in the opus regulatum style (a regular grid pattern) whereas the Pompeii mosaic is in the opus palladianum style (the tesserae vary in size and shape and are placed haphazardly).

Class activities

- Let the children select one of the marine creatures to draw on the grid on their A4 paper (or hand them out according to ability).
- Ask the children to fill the entire grid rather than leaving too much space around the drawing and to copy lines and shapes; show them your example.
- The children should use light pencil marks to copy the sea creature onto their grid.

Plenary

Gather the children to look at their drawings so far and highlight where children have successfully managed to create a full composition, i.e. one which fills the page. Use your pre-prepared drawing and explain to the children that they will next need to paint their drawing. Show the children how the Pompeii mosaic includes detail and shades and tints, which make it more realistic. Demonstrate to the children how to begin with an original colour and gradually add black to make shades or white to make tints.

Lesson 2 Tints and shades

Key artwork

Pompeii, *Sea Creature Mosaic*, first century AD

You will need
- A4 images of marine creatures
- A4 paper with grid and the children's drawings from the previous lesson
- Pencils
- Erasers
- Watercolour paints
- Thin and medium brushes
- Water pots
- Tissues for dabbing
- Glue stick
- Scissors
- Aprons

Preparation

Paint some or all of the examples you prepared for last lesson, including details, shades and tints.

Getting started

Look at the key artwork and remind the children about how the mosaic is made up of tesserae and how the artist has included details and shades and tints to make the overall image more realistic. Look at some of the marine images that the children have been copying and bring their attention to the details that they should endeavour to reproduce. Recap with the children how to begin with an original colour and make it darker or lighter.

Class activities
- Let the children complete their drawings if they need to.
- Allow the children to spend time painting their marine creature, using the original image as a guide.

Plenary

Gather the children to look at their paintings. Highlight examples where the artist has used a range of tints and shades and included a lot of details. Ask the children if they can work out what the next step will be in making the mosaic. Reveal that the children will need to cut and stick the tesserae next.

Lesson 3 Mosaic making

Key artwork
Anonymous, *Sea Creature Mosaic*, first century AD

You will need
- A4 images of marine creatures
- A4 paper with grid and the children's paintings from the previous lesson
- Watercolour paints
- Thin and medium brushes
- Water pots
- Tissues for dabbing
- Glue sticks
- Scissors
- Backing paper in any colour
- Aprons

Preparation
Lay the materials out so that the children can access them. Have your painted example ready so that you can demonstrate how to cut squares and stick them onto the backing paper.

Getting started
Look at the key artwork and bring the children's attention to the spaces in-between the tesserae; explain that the gaps are important to create the overall mosaic look. Look at how the Pompeii mosaic is created using different sizes and shapes of tesserae that move in different directions. Explain that to make the process more straightforward, the children are using a simple grid with even rows and columns. Demonstrate how to use the gridlines to cut your painting one row at a time, then cut each square and stick it one at a time to the backing paper and create a mosaic. Be sure to leave a gap in-between the tesserae and keep the rows and columns in line with each other. Do not cut the whole image up at once as this will cause confusion when trying to put the mosaic together.

Class activities
- Let the children complete their paintings if needed.
- The children should now cut their paintings row by row using the gridlines.
- After cutting each row the children should cut square by square and stick as they cut, leaving gaps between each tesserae.

Plenary
Gather the children to look at their mosaics. Ask the children to comment on each other's work using the specific vocabulary learnt. Ask the children to comment on the challenges of creating a mosaic and reflect on how skilled the mosaic artist was that made the Pompeii sea creature mosaic.

Further activities

1. The children could combine their paintings to make one large mosaic or they could each replicate a creature from the original Pompeii mosaic. They could make a mosaic that is a menu of food available to them now, in the same way that the Pompeii mosaic showed available marine life.

Cross-curricular links

Science: This could work well alongside learning about animals and habitats – the children could research the marine life that they are depicting.

History: The children could create this mosaic alongside learning about Pompeii and Roman life – they could look more closely at the *Alexandra Mosaic*.

14 Aboriginal dot paintings: Using symbols

In 30 seconds...

In these lessons, the children will learn about the indigenous people of Australia, their approach to dot painting and the use of symbols in their art. The children will use a combination of aboriginal symbols and their own to create a dot painting.

Key artwork

Walangkura Napanangka, *Tjintjintjin*, acrylic on linen, date unknown. (There are two images by this artist of the same name, either is fine.)

What do I need to know?

The Aboriginal people are the indigenous people of Australia. Experts believe they came to Australia around 45,000 years ago. There is still a diminished Aboriginal population in Australia but their traditional lifestyle has suffered greatly since the European invasion in the 1700s.

Prior to the arrival of Europeans, Australia was home to several clans of Aboriginal people who spoke different languages and had their own territories. The highest population of Aborigines was along the coast, where they could fish and hunt to sustain a good lifestyle. Those that lived inland could hunt and gather, and clans would move when needed and according to the seasons. The Aborigines had sufficient time for leisure and they enjoyed a rich cultural and spiritual life, including distinctive regional artistic styles. Their lives were principally rooted in respect for nature and the land. The European invasions had detrimental effects on the Aboriginal people: their land was appropriated and lethal diseases that the people could not withstand spread, often with devastating outcomes. The invaders did not seek to understand the Aboriginal way of life, belief systems or rituals and instead dismissed Aboriginal culture as primitive and uncivilised. Aboriginal culture was destroyed and the people were encouraged to assimilate white European ways of life. Although there are still Aborigines in Australia, the post-invasion Aboriginal population has diminished and much of the traditional way of life is gone.

Much of Aboriginal culture was passed on orally, through storytelling, dance and art. A significant inspiration for art and culture was something known as the 'Dreamtime'. The Dreamtime is part of the Aboriginal belief system that explains how everything was created by ancestral spirits. There are many stories that explain how various creatures and landscapes came into being throughout the Dreamtime. Despite broad interpretations, some of the specifics about the Dreamtime and its spirits vary amongst the different tribes, just as Aboriginal art differs in style and character.

Evidence of old Aboriginal paintings has been found in Australian caves, engraved onto rocks and painted onto tree bark, but there continues to be Aboriginal artists working in Australia today, producing traditional and contemporary paintings. Examples of styles of Aboriginal painting are 'x-ray painting', 'cross-hatching', 'dot painting' and sometimes a combination of styles.

X-ray paintings depict humans and animals with their internal organs and bones visible – examples of these types of paintings have been found on cave walls. Aboriginal bark paintings often include cross-hatching; the effect is achieved using strands of hair dipped into the paint and laid onto the desired surface. Dot painting is perhaps the style most widely associated with Aboriginal art and it produces bold, eye-catching effects. Before canvas or manufactured paint, Aboriginal people would make drawings in the earth to illustrate their tales of the Dreamtime. These designs were transient, disappearing with a wipe of the hand or fading in the wind. Modern dot paintings are more permanent as the designs and techniques became translated into mediums such as canvas and acrylic paints, and dot paintings could therefore reach a wider audience.

Although Aboriginal people do not have their own written language, they do make use of common symbols and these are frequently seen in paintings. Artists like Walangkura Napanangka (1946–2014) use combinations of these symbols to tell stories through their artwork. Napanangka was one of the last of a generation who recalled a more traditional way of life, hunting and gathering, living in the deserts with her father and mother. When she was just a teenager, the family trekked on foot across hundreds of kilometres, to reach a settlement and begin a new life. The settlement promised an easier way of life with resources more readily available, but there were also many adjustments to lifestyle. Napanangka has enjoyed great success as a commercial artist; she has been involved in many exhibitions and her work is held in international gallery collections.

- The **Aborigines** are the **indigenous** people of Australia.
- Aboriginal people enjoyed a rich cultural and spiritual life and lived off the land as fishermen, hunters and gatherers.
- Aboriginal people believe in the **Dreamtime**, and much of their storytelling is inspired by stories about creation.
- After the European invasion in the 1700s, the traditional Aboriginal way of life suffered and never fully recovered.
- Aboriginal people lost much of their land and became ill as they could not fight European diseases, and were forced to give up their traditions.
- The Aboriginal population declined after the European invasion.
- Aboriginal painting comes in **regional** styles and often uses **symbols** to tell stories.
- There is a contemporary Aboriginal art scene and many artists combine traditional styles such as **x-ray painting, cross-hatching** and **dot painting** with contemporary approaches.

Vocabulary

Aborigines: The indigenous people of Australia.
Cross-hatching: Shading with lines that cross over.
Dot painting: Painting made using dots rather than brush strokes.
Dreamtime: Ancient time of the creation of all things, as part of the Aboriginal belief system.
Indigenous: Originating from a place.
Regional: Relating to a particular area.
Symbols: Something used to represent something else.

Useful links

www.kateowengallery.com Website to find the key artwork
www.japingkaaboriginalart.com/articles/facts-about-aboriginal-art Information about aboriginal art

Lesson 1 Symbols

Key artwork

Walangkura Napanangka, *Tjintjintjin*, acrylic on linen

You will need

- A worksheet of a selection of Aboriginal symbols, see **Bloomsbury Online Resource 14A**
- A3 or A4 paper in earth colours
- Pencils
- Erasers
- Scrap paper
- Cotton bud
- Acrylic or poster paint
- Aprons

Preparation

Use an Internet search to find a suitable example of a Dreamtime story that you can share with the children and a selection of aboriginal symbols for making a worksheet – both are easily found by searching key words such as *Dreamtime story* and *aboriginal symbols*.

Getting started

Look at the key artwork and ask the children if they have any ideas about where this work is from or who the artist is. Discuss with the children the techniques that they think the artist used and whether they think the painting has a narrative or not. Explain the background of the key artwork and ask the children if they can share any modern symbols, e.g. street signs or maths symbols. Show the children the worksheet containing symbols and their meanings and explain how the Aboriginals used these symbols to tell stories, often of the Dreamtime. Explain that the children will be making their own dot painting using traditional Aboriginal symbols, and they can use the symbols to create their own stories in their art.

Class activities

- Let the children use the symbols worksheet and draw their design in light pencil.
- The story does not have to be comprehensive but the children should consider their composition and the overall look of their design.

Plenary

Gather the children to look at their designs, ask them to share any stories that they developed using the symbols and encourage them to share tips for improving their compositions. Ask the children if they have any ideas about how to develop the design using paint and in the dot style. Explain to the children than they will be using cotton buds and demonstrate to them how to hold the bud vertically and press the paint so as to achieve a clear dot shape.

Lesson 2 Dot painting

Key artwork
Walangkura Napanangka, *Tjintjintjin*, acrylic on linen

You will need
- A worksheet of a selection of Aboriginal symbols, see **Bloomsbury Online Resource 14A**
- The children's work from the previous lesson
- Pencils
- Erasers
- Scrap paper
- Cotton buds
- Acrylic or poster paint in palettes with a few of the cotton buds in each colour
- Aprons

Preparation
Fill the palettes with paint and carefully lay cotton buds next to the colours.

Getting started
Look at the key artwork and recap with the children how to use the cotton buds to achieve a clear dot mark. Tell them that they can vary the gaps in-between the dots to achieve different effects. Explain that the children should not mix the cotton buds to ensure that the colours stay clean.

Class activities
- Let the children use the cotton buds and paint to place dots along the design that they created in the last lesson.
- Encourage the children to share tips with each other about how to keep the dots clear, e.g. not rushing, pressing firmly and holding the bud upright rather than at an angle.

Plenary
Gather the children to look at their designs. Ask them to share their stories and encourage them to share tips for improving their painting.

Lesson 3 Dot painting story

Key artwork
Walangkura Napanangka, *Tjintjintjin*, acrylic on linen

You will need
- A worksheet of a selection of Aboriginal symbols, see **Bloomsbury Online Resource 14A**
- The children's work from the previous lesson
- Scrap paper
- Cotton buds
- Acrylic or poster paint in palettes with a few of the cotton buds in each colour
- Pencils
- Aprons

Preparation
Fill the palettes with paint and carefully lay cotton buds next to the colours.

Getting started
Look at the key artwork and recap with the children how to use the cotton buds to achieve a clear dot mark. Tell them that they can vary the gaps in-between the dots to achieve different effects. Remind the children not to mix the cotton buds to ensure that the colours stay clean. Look at the children's paintings from the previous lesson and spend some time ensuring that the compositions are full and interesting. Give the children time to add symbols with a pencil if they need to.

Class activities
- Let the children use the cotton buds and paint to place dots along their design.
- Encourage the children to share tips with each other about how to keep the dots clear, e.g. not rushing, pressing firmly and holding the bud upright rather than at an angle.
- Encourage the children to step back from their work to see where they need to add more dots to fill blank spaces

Plenary
Gather the children to look at their designs. Ask them to share their stories and encourage them to share tips for improving their painting. Look at more examples of Aboriginal art and ask the children to discuss how they think it compares to paintings of a different style – select a style that the children know as an example to compare with, e.g. the Impressionist style.

Further activities

1. The children could spend more time learning Dreamtime stories and make paintings to illustrate them.
2. They could develop their own symbols and make a dot painting that tells a story about a tradition that they observe.

Cross-curricular links

Maths: The children could use their knowledge of shapes to help them to develop their own symbols.

History: The children could create this mosaic alongside learning about the Aboriginals.

English: The children could write the stories to go with their paintings.

15 Albrecht Dürer: Visual texture

In 30 seconds...

*In these lessons the children will look at the print **Rhinoceros** by Dürer, and learn about the interesting story of the animal depicted in it. They will explore ways of showing visual texture using lines, shapes and tones to depict animals.*

Key artwork

Albrecht Dürer, *Rhinoceros*, woodcut, 1515

What do I need to know?

Albrecht Dürer (1471–1528) was a master artist of the German Renaissance period. Dürer was a painter, draughtsman and writer but he is possibly best known as a printmaker, he used a combination of lines impeccably to depict the surface texture of the things he drew. Dürer believed that every work of art, whether a self-portrait or not, informed the viewer about the artist's personality. This was a new concept for that time, and many experts credit Dürer as the first to bring about the idea of the artist's character as a subject of interest. Dürer was possibly one of the first recorded to produce a nude self-portrait in 1509, and the first to create a sketch of himself sketching – a composition taken on by other artists since, such as M.C. Escher.

Dürer lived in the German city of Nuremberg during a golden age. It was a busy trade city and was held in high esteem for its commercial and cultural output. It was known as a quintessential medieval city with many thriving craft industries. Dürer's father was a goldsmith and as such would have been one of the most respected craftspeople in the city. Drawing was key to the goldsmith trade and Dürer mastered the art very early on, demonstrating great natural talent at a young age.

The key artwork is a print that has become an iconic image from European history; it was one of the first mass produced images in Europe. The animal in the print was the first rhinoceros to reach Europe; it hailed from Gujarat in India and was given to the King of Portugal as a gift from the Portuguese governor in India. It arrived in Lisbon in 1515 to a great fanfare. The news of this exotic creature spread and was especially well received as this was an age when people were thirsty for knowledge of faraway lands. Pre-technology, verbal descriptions would have been the only way to conjure up the imagery to share news about the animal, and Albrecht Dürer heard a description of the rhinoceros when he was living in Nuremberg. He was immediately compelled to depict it and he used a rough sketch and description from a friend to make his woodblock drawing. If you look closely at the image, you can see that Dürer has interpreted his eyewitness's description as best he could and possibly combined it with his knowledge of other animals, but the print is not entirely accurate. The rhinoceros in Dürer's print has scales and two horns, unlike an actual rhinoceros, and it has a tortoise-like shell reminiscent of human armour. The eyes are human-like and it has wisps of fur on its ears and chin that are not dissimilar to those found on a dog.

By 1515, when the print was made, Dürer was already a very prestigious artist and he was also the first artist to have his own printing press. By producing a print (rather than a painting or drawing of the rhinoceros) and making it available to the public, Dürer was ensuring that his work would be sought after by a wide audience who were keen to own a picture of this new curiosity. The woodcut ensured a level of financial security for the artist and Dürer elevated the woodblock print to new heights by exploiting the use of shading, detail hatching, and lines to show the different visual textures on the animal.

- Dürer was a painter, **draughtsman** and writer but he is possibly best known as a printmaker.
- The city of Nuremberg where Dürer lived, was a thriving place with many highly skilled **craftspeople** – Dürer's father was a **goldsmith**.
- The key artwork is a print and has become an **iconic** image from European history; it was one of the first **mass-produced** images in Europe.
- At a young age, Dürer demonstrated artistic talent.
- The rhinoceros in the print was the first to arrive in Europe and it arrived in Lisbon as a gift to the then Portuguese king in 1515 – people across Europe were extremely curious about the exotic animal.
- **Verbal** descriptions would have been the only way for people to visualise the rhinoceros and news of the animal reached Nuremberg in Germany.
- When Dürer heard about the animal from a friend, he wanted to make an image for all to see.
- Dürer was already an accomplished artist with a good reputation and he was the first artist to own his own **printing press**, and he used his situation to produce and successfully sell many copies of the Lisbon rhinoceros print.
- Although a good likeness, Dürer has not made a totally accurate depiction of the animal. He has used some artistic licence as well as his prior knowledge of other animals to create the woodblock.
- Dürer skilfully used the woodblock to create an image that shows different **visual textures**. He exploits the potential of lines and shapes to show details and shades.

Vocabulary

Craftspeople: People skilled at making things.
Draughtsman: A person skilled in drawing.
Goldsmith: A person who makes items out of gold.
Mass-produced: The production or manufacture of goods in large quantities.
Printing press: A machine for printing text or pictures from plates or woodblocks.
Verbal: Expressed in spoken words.
Visual texture: A representation of texture that an artist creates using line, tone and colour.

Useful links

www.youtube.com/watch?v=IPthhO4YU28 Video about the artwork
www.albrecht-durer.org/Rhinoceros-large.html *Rhinoceros*

Lesson 1 Visual texture

Key artwork
Albrecht Dürer, *Rhinoceros*, woodcut, 1515

You will need
- A3 paper folded into eight sections
- Pencils
- Erasers
- Eight small canvas bags or covered containers, each bag filled with a different texture, e.g. cotton wool, tinfoil, straws, silk, tinsel, sand and rocks

Preparation
Before the lesson, you will need to prepare the eight bags or containers, filling them with different materials and ensuring that the children will not be able to see through the container to work out what is inside. You will need to number the bags clearly 1–8, so that the children can clearly see which number bag they are feeling. As there are eight bags, it is useful to separate the children into eight smaller groups of three or four, so that the bags can be rotated around the room – they can remain in their seats so long as they know who is in their group. It is much easier if you fold the A3 paper before the lesson, unless you want to include a mini lesson on folding with the children.

Getting started
Look at the key artwork and ask the children to discuss what they can see, encourage the children to look at the image and spot any clues about how old it is, i.e. the style of German script at the top and the date. Explain to the children the story surrounding the Lisbon rhinoceros and ask them if they think it is a true representation of the animal; if not, ask them to identify any inaccuracies. Zoom in on sections of the rhinoceros and explain that Dürer tried to convey the texture of the skin, discuss what texture is and that artists try to show it to make their work more realistic. Ask the children to comment on how they think the artist drew textures and then explain that he used different types of lines and shapes. Tell the children what is meant by visual texture, you could demonstrate by drawing a rough zig-zag line on paper and showing how it doesn't feel spikey but it *looks* like it does. Explain that the children will be trying to show visual textures using lines and shapes, encourage the children to share some examples of lines and shapes they might use for different textures, e.g. a long wavy line to show a smooth texture or lots of small dashes for a prickly texture.

Class activities
- Give the children their paper and ask them to write small numbers in their boxes, 1–8.
- Show the children the bags, pointing out that the bags are numbered 1–8 like their boxes and telling them that the texture drawing should go in the correct box i.e. the box with the same number as the bag.
- Tell the children that each bag contains a mystery texture and that each time they put their hands into a bag they will feel something different.
- Demonstrate how to look at the bag number, feel inside the bag, think about the texture and

then use lines and shapes to draw in the corresponding box. It is useful if in your demonstration, you think out loud, saying words to describe the texture and before drawing in the correct box.
- You will need to oversee the bags being passed to the eight groups of children. The idea is that by the end of the task, the children have felt eight different textures and filled the eight boxes on their paper.

Plenary
Gather the children with their drawings and ask them to use descriptive words to talk about the different textures that they can see in each other's work. Ask the children if they can guess what was in the bags. Then reveal the contents.

Lesson 2 Drawing from descriptions 1

Key artwork
Albrecht Dürer, *Rhinoceros*, woodcut, 1515

You will need
- A3 or A4 paper
- Images of different animals from around the world – the more obscure the better – enough for one each
- Pencils
- Erasers

Preparation
Source and print images of a variety of animals, you will need one for each child. If duplicating, then make sure children working in a pair have different images.

Getting started
Look at the key artwork and recap how Dürer created the drawing based largely on a verbal description from a friend. Explain that the children will be working in pairs to create drawings that depict animals from around the world. Distribute a picture to one child in each pair – they must not show their partner the picture. Explain the task: the child with the picture must use words to describe the animal whilst their partner draws it. The child who is doing the describing should describe the texture and details of the animal, but must not say the name of the animal. It is permissible to refer to other animals to help the verbal description, e.g. 'It has a neck like a giraffe but thinner and with no fur'. The idea is for the artist to create a drawing that is as detailed as possible and shows a variety of visual textures.

Class activities
- Let the children work in pairs to begin the drawing task – they will swap next lesson.
- Encourage the children to use a range of vocabulary to describe their animal to the artist.

Plenary

Gather the children with their drawings. Ask the class to look at the drawings and try and guess what animal each artist was being told about. Look at good examples of the artist using lines and shapes to show the textures.

Lesson 3 Drawing from descriptions II

Key artwork

Albrecht Dürer, *Rhinoceros*, woodcut, 1515

You will need

- A3 or A4 paper
- The images of different animals from around the world from last lesson
- Pencils
- Erasers

Preparation

Make sure that the children sit next to the same partner as last lesson.

Getting started

Look at the key artwork and recap how Dürer created the drawing based largely on a verbal description from a friend. Explain that the children will be swapping roles and working in the same pairs as last lesson to create drawings that depict animals from around the world. As last lesson, the child doing the describing must use words to describe the animal whilst their partner draws it. The child describing the animal should describe the texture and details of the animal in his/her picture but must not say the name of the animal. It is permissible to refer to other animals to help the verbal description, e.g. 'It has a neck like a giraffe but thinner and with no fur'. The idea is for the artist to create a drawing that is as detailed as possible and shows a variety of visual textures.

Class activities

- Let the children work in pairs to begin the drawing task.
- Encourage the children to use a range of vocabulary to describe their animal to the artist.

Plenary

Gather the children with their drawings and ask the class to look at the drawings and try to guess what animal each artist was being told about. Look at good examples of the artist using lines and shapes to show the textures. Ask the children to reflect on how difficult it was to draw from a description.

Further activities

1. The children could develop these drawings into prints using foam or polystyrene tiles.
2. The children could develop the drawings into paintings, showing textures and colours.

Cross-curricular links

History: The children could study Europe in the 1500s alongside this scheme.

Part 3
Upper Key Stage 2

What does the KS2 curriculum say?

Pupils should be taught:

- to create sketchbooks to record their observations and use them to review and revisit ideas
- to improve their mastery of art and design techniques, including drawing, painting and sculpture with a range of materials [for example, pencil, charcoal, paint, clay]
- about great artists, architects and designers in history.

Curriculum content

By the end of KS2, children should feel confident using a range of techniques and materials and they should be able to do so with a level of competency and control that is distinctly higher than lower KS2 children. Through directed tasks and exploratory learning, the children will learn to use different materials with intention, to achieve desired outcomes and effects. The children should also feel confident taking risks with their ideas and approaches, experimenting in sketchbooks or through preparatory work on paper to discover new creative outcomes. They will continue to develop skills in painting, drawing, collage, printing and sculpture, building on prior learning.

Throughout upper KS2 the children are exposed to a dynamic range of artists and styles, even developing their own conceptual artwork with their choice of artistic medium. These works will challenge and extend the children's idea about what is considered art and what the purpose of art is. They will learn about artists who make work about issues that might challenge their perceptions of the world, and they will come to understand how art can help to raise awareness of important events and subjects, and even how artists can be pioneers.

The children should be encouraged to have lively debate and discussion about artists and key artworks and by now should be able to share opinions about art in an articulate way, obviously to varying degrees. Alluding to the arrangement of the formal elements in their own and others' work should be an expectation. You may want to extend the analysis of art to include some writing tasks, and the children should certainly be able to share verbally the concepts behind their own work and the processes and techniques used to create them.

16 Antoni Gaudí: Architecture and design

In 30 seconds...

In these lessons, the children will look at the architecture of Gaudí and learn how he was inspired by natural forms. They will use images of their school or a regularly visited building and transform it using influences from natural forms and Gaudí's work.

Key artwork

Antoni Gaudí, *Sagrada Família*, Barcelona, Spain

What do I need to know?

Antoni Gaudí (1852–1926) was a Spanish architect. Gaudí's first commission was for street lamps but he soon established himself, and today the city of Barcelona is occupied by many instantly recognisable Gaudí buildings. Gaudí's style was influenced by nature, often incorporating colours, patterns, organic forms and curved lines as opposed to the usual geometric shapes found in buildings. Gaudí studied architecture in Barcelona and he graduated in 1878. He was extremely proud of his Catalonian heritage and his work celebrated this as well as being influenced by the Modernisme movement that was prevalent in Catalonia at that time. Catalonian culture was experiencing a renaissance and key members of the region wanted to lift Catalonian culture to the same status as that in other European cities. Modernisme was closely related to the English Arts and Crafts Movement, which included artists such as William Morris (see Chapter 20). There were related movements happening in other European cities too. These movements engaged many of the prominent bohemian intellectuals of the day, and the style influenced not just art and craft but music, prose and poetry too. Barcelona has one of the strongest architectural legacies of this time though, due largely to the work of Gaudí. The Gothic revival was also a strong influence on Gaudí and his contemporaries; creatives began to look to the medieval period for design inspiration, as a reaction to the neoclassical style that was becoming popular, where design was influenced by ancient civilisations. That said, Gaudí's style is hard to define and his buildings are eccentric and individualistic.

The *Sagrada Família* is Gaudí's best-known work, and is a UNESCO world heritage site. Gaudí was an extremely devout Catholic and his aim was to depict the history of the Catholic faith in a building, as well as to make an offering to counteract what he saw as the sins of modern living. Gaudí became obsessed with the building and towards the end of his life he lost all interest in anything else – it is said that he neglected his appearance so much that he was often mistaken for a tramp and would even sleep on site to be closer to his work. Gaudí wanted the interior of the building to feel like a forest, as he believed it was in nature that a person could feel closer to God. Gaudí was aware that the building would not be able to reach completion in his lifetime so he created a set of complicated models and designs to ensure that the church could be finished how he envisaged it. Gaudí died in a tram accident in 1926 and the building was left unfinished, but the designs left by Gaudí guided builders for the next ten years. In 1936 rebels destroyed the models that Gaudí had left behind and architects and builders have continued to try and use these broken pieces to guide them. Today, modern technology has meant that the construction process is much more efficient, and completion is set for 2020–2030.

- Antoni Gaudí was a Spanish **architect**.
- Gaudí's approach was influenced by the creative movements of the time as well as his own **individualistic artistic style**.
- Gaudí's buildings are recognisable, often because they include **organic forms** and curved lines, in **contrast** with more conventional buildings.
- The *Sagrada Família* is Gaudí's most renowned building; it is in the centre of Barcelona.
- It is thanks to Gaudí's **design** work that the building of the *Sagrada Família* has been able to be continued long after his death.

Vocabulary

Architect: A person who designs buildings and often supervises the construction.
Artistic style: A distinctive way of working, which can permit grouping of works.
Design: A plan or drawing made to depict the look and function or workings of a building, garment, or another object before it is made.
Individualistic: Being characteristic of that person.
Organic forms: In art, shapes that are often flowing and unpredictable in contrast to geometric shapes.

Useful links

www.sagradafamilia.org/en Official *Sagrada Família* website

Lesson 1 Sketching natural forms

Key artwork
Antoni Gaudí, *Sagrada Família*, Barcelona, Spain

You will need
- Natural forms such as shells and pine cones, etc.
- Pencils
- Erasers
- A3 paper, one for each child
- Slideshow and handout with a selection of Gaudí's buildings on them, including details

Preparation

Gather a selection of images of Gaudí's buildings, including details of rooftops, stairwells, etc. Present these on a slideshow as well as printing them out as handouts. Collect a variety of natural forms.

Getting started

Ask the children to tell you what an architect is and discuss the buildings that they know and like. Find out if any of the children have visited Barcelona and ask them to share what they remember, then tell the children they will be learning about a Spanish architect. Show the children the key artwork and tell the children about Gaudí and his work. Show the other images of Gaudí's buildings on the slideshow/handout to emphasise that he was inspired by natural forms. Ask the children if they can see the connection between any of the buildings and natural forms, e.g. staircases like shells, the inside of the *Sagrada Família* like a forest, tops of chimneys like bluebells, etc. Explain that the children will be redesigning the school building (or other building that they visit regularly) to look like one of Gaudí's buildings. Tell them they must first collect some sketches of natural forms.

Class activities

- Give the children a selection of natural forms and ask them to make sketches of them. Explain that they do not have to make detailed drawings; the sketches should capture the shapes and lines so that these can be used for a building design.

Plenary

Gather the children with their drawings and discuss whether any of the natural forms inspired any ideas for buildings. Encourage the children to use their imaginations to make links between their drawings and features of a building.

Lesson 2 Designing

Key artwork

Antoni Gaudí, *Sagrada Família*, Barcelona, Spain

You will need

- Children's artwork from the previous lesson
- A4 photographs of the school building (or other chosen building), enough for one each – some complicated and some of larger more simple details – these should be as light as possible so the children can draw over the top
- Pencils
- Erasers
- Black fine liner pens

Preparation

Use one of the photographs of the building and some of the children's sketches of natural forms, and combine the two, superimposing features of the natural forms onto the photograph. You can adjust the scale and repeat lines and forms to redesign the building, e.g. you could use the spiral from a shell to redesign an external staircase or the wavy lines from a pine cone could frame a window.

Getting started

Look at the children's sketches from the last lesson alongside the images of the school building (or other chosen building). Discuss with the children how they could combine their sketches to redesign the building. Give an example of how you might use a line or shape from a natural form sketch and draw it over the top of the photograph, e.g. a shell shape could form a window. Show your example and then demonstrate how you looked through the sketches to find appropriate shapes to superimpose onto the photograph, explain how you selected parts rather than just copying the whole sketch onto the photograph.

Class activities

- The children should now begin to draw over the top of the photographs with a pencil, using the natural form sketches to inform their decisions.
- When the children are satisfied with their designs, they can go over the basic lines and shapes of the whole photograph, including their embellishments, with the black pen.

Plenary

Gather the children with their designs and discuss which ones are successful and why. Show the children how they will next use A4 tracing paper to trace over the black lines, leaving them with a redesign of the building.

Lesson 3 Final design

Key artwork

Antoni Gaudí, *Sagrada Família*, Barcelona, Spain

You will need

- The children's natural form drawings from the previous lesson
- The photographs of the school building (or other chosen building) with the children's additional design features
- A4 tracing paper, one each
- Black fine liner pens
- Coloured felt tip pens

Preparation

Use your example from last lesson, place the tracing paper over the top and trace the black lines. It is useful to do this for just half of the work so that you can demonstrate the tracing the other half in front of the children.

Getting started

Demonstrate to the children how they can place the tracing paper over the top of the photograph of the school building (or other chosen building) and then trace the basic lines and shapes, including their natural form additions. The children will be left with a piece of tracing paper that has the basic outlines of the building with the addition of natural form features. They can add colour to the tracing paper using felt tip pens; encourage them to be adventurous with colour and refer to Gaudí's buildings.

Class activities

• The children should now trace over their photograph and add colour to their final design.

Plenary

Gather the children with their designs and discuss which designs have been successful and which look instantly recognisable as a Gaudí inspired building. Ask the children to share any other ideas they have for buildings, not necessarily inspired by natural forms.

Further activities

1. The children could redesign the school freehand, i.e. without the use of the tracing paper.
2. They could also develop their idea into a miniature 3D model of the building.

Cross-curricular links

Maths: The children could be given actual measurements of the building and be asked to scale down measurements for their designs.
Geography: This could form part of a topic on people and places in Spain.

17 Chris Ofili: Conceptual art

In 30 seconds...

In these lessons, the children will look at the work of Chris Ofili and learn about the concept behind it. They will come to understand how some contemporary artists work initially with concepts and then develop visual work to present those ideas. The children will select an idea or issue that is interesting to them and develop a piece of conceptual work that represents those ideas, working independently to create their practical work.

Note: The key artwork will require some sensitive discussion as it involves a historic news story that some might find difficult to discuss. The key artwork could be substituted with another conceptual piece, e.g. Rachel Whiteread's *House*, or Anish Kapoor's *As if to Celebrate, I Discovered a Mountain Blooming with Flowers*.

> ### Key artwork
>
> Chris Ofili, *No Woman, No Cry*, 1998, oil paint, acrylic paint, graphite, polyester resin, printed paper, glitter, map pins and elephant dung on canvas

What do I need to know?

In 1998, Chris Ofili (born 1968) won the Turner Prize, an art award given annually to a British artist under fifty. The Turner Prize began in 1984 and every year it receives much publicity; it gives the public an insight into the goings-on in contemporary British art. Nominees and winners often exhibit work that is controversial and which spurs discussions about what is considered art. Much of the artwork exhibited as part of the Turner prize is installation, sculpture, video or performance art. Chris Ofili's work was the first painting to win since 1985. Many contemporary artists' work is conceptual and therefore the artists are free to use whatever medium they see fit to represent their concept. Chris Ofili was part of a popular group of artists in the late nineties, called the Young British Artists.

No Woman, No Cry is a large mixed-media painting that depicts a woman in profile. The woman is crying and if you look closely you will see that inside each of her tears is a small photograph of a boy. The painting's surface is textured and tactile; it has layered patterns and decorations. The artist has not painted a realistic portrait but has chosen to show the lady in a particular style. Although the lady is crying, she is holding her head high and there is an air of dignity about her. The lady is Doreen Lawrence (now Baroness Lawrence of Clarendon, OBE), she was the mother of Stephen Lawrence. Stephen was a teenager when he was tragically murdered in 1993 and although Chris Ofili did not know the Lawrence family, he like the rest of the country, was deeply saddened by the event. The newspapers and news reports at the time were covering controversies surrounding the murder and the fact that it was a racist attack. Ofili was moved by images and stories of Doreen Lawrence, and her grief and loss is depicted in his work.

Chris Ofili is known for combining different materials and using elephant dung in his work. *No Woman, No Cry* is propped up on this unusual material and Doreen Lawrence wears an elephant dung pendant around her neck. The painting also has the letters 'RIP' painted in bioluminescent paint, seen most clearly at night, although you can faintly see the layer of paint during the day. The title of the painting takes its name from a well-known Bob Marley song.

- **Contemporary art** is often **conceptual** and can be **controversial**.
- The **Turner Prize** promotes contemporary British artists and Chris Ofili won this prize with his painting *No Woman, No Cry*.
- Conceptual artists can work in a range of mediums, sometimes **non-traditional**.
- Conceptual artworks often make the most sense when you read about the artist's ideas and then look at the artwork.
- Often **unconventional** artworks are made to **represent** the artists' **concept**.

Vocabulary

Concept: An idea.
Conceptual: Based on ideas.
Contemporary art: Art that is produced in the present day or in the recent past.
Controversial: Causing disagreement and dividing opinion.
Non-traditional: Not according to the usual traditions.
Represent: To stand for or symbolise.
Turner Prize: An art award given every year to a British artist.
Unconventional: Not the usual.

Useful links

www.tate.org.uk/art/artworks/ofili-no-woman-no-cry-t07502/text-summary Chris Ofili's work on the Tate website
www.tate.org.uk/art/art-terms/c/conceptual-art Tate definition and examples of conceptual art

Lesson 1 Concepts

Key artwork
Chris Ofili, *No Woman, No Cry*, 1998, oil paint, acrylic paint, graphite, polyester resin, printed paper, glitter, map pins and elephant dung on canvas

You will need
- A3 paper
- Pencils
- Colouring pencils
- Felt tips

Preparation
Make an example of a mind map of issues or topics that interest you. This should demonstrate to the children how mind maps can connect ideas and include sketches and words.

Getting started
Ask the children to discuss the question 'What is art?'. Explain that this is a question that many people ask, especially when it comes to contemporary artwork. Tell the children about the Turner Prize and introduce them to Chris Ofili's work, being sure to leave time for sensitive discussions about the issues that come up from the painting. At an appropriate time, move on to discuss how contemporary artists often make their art about their ideas or an issue that moves them. Ask the children to think about and discuss things that are important to them, e.g. ideas they find themselves thinking about (however wacky), news issues that have interested them and people, activities and things that are important to them. Show the children your example and talk them through your ideas.

Class activities
- The children should now use the A3 paper to create a mind map of their ideas. They should write and draw lists of issues, ideas and important people and things in their lives. This does not have to look any particular way; describe it to the children as emptying their brains out onto the paper.
- Ask the children to pick their top idea from the mind map and ask them to write down the first ten words or pictures that come to mind when they think about it.
- Ask the children to share their top idea verbally with the class.

Plenary
Gather the children and ask them to share how it felt to just write ideas and thoughts in that way. Explain that next week the children will begin to sketch and make their concepts, and suggest that they begin to think about how they might represent their idea. Tell the children that they can collect materials for their idea to bring in for next lesson.

Lesson 2 Representing an idea

Key artwork
Chris Ofili, *No Woman, No Cry*, 1998, oil paint, acrylic paint, graphite, polyester resin, printed paper, glitter, map pins and elephant dung on canvas

You will need
- The children's mind maps from the last lesson
- A range of materials, including any the children have brought in, e.g. paints, collage materials, felt tips, glue, oil pastels
- Paper in a range of sizes, the children can select the appropriate size for their work

Preparation
Ensure that the materials are clearly labelled and easy to access as the children will be working independently to select what they need. You could prepare a list of all the materials that will be available to the children and allow them to look at the list to select which they want to use before physically getting the materials.

Getting started
Ask some of the children to describe their selected concept and their thoughts about how to represent it. Explain that today the children will begin to make their conceptual art. Remind them that they should be able to describe the concept using words, both verbal and written.

Class activities
- Ask the children to write a sentence or two that explains their concept. If some children are stuck for ideas, allow them to choose a person that is important to them and make a portrait from their memory.
- The children can select the appropriately sized paper to produce their outcome.
- Allow the children to use any of the materials provided or that they have brought in to make their work. If you are limited with materials and space, give the children a list of materials that are available to them first, so they can make a materials list.

Plenary
Allow the children to present their concepts to the class and show their practical work so far.

Lesson 3 Conceptual art

Key artwork
Chris Ofili, *No Woman, No Cry*, 1998, oil paint, acrylic paint, graphite, polyester resin, printed paper, glitter, map pins and elephant dung on canvas

You will need
- The children's mind maps and work in progress from the last lesson

- A comprehensive range of materials, including any the children have brought in, e.g. paints, collage materials, felt tips, glue, oil pastels, newspaper articles
- Paper in a range of sizes

Preparation
Ensure that the materials are clearly labelled and easy to access as the children will be working independently to select what they need.

Getting started
Remind the children that using the materials independently is part of acting like an artist. Recap what is meant by a conceptual artist and remind the children that their practical work should represent their concept.

Class activities
- Allow the children time to complete their conceptual artwork.

Plenary
Allow the children to show their practical work and include with it the sentence that describes their concepts. Ask the children to share their favourite pieces and explain why.

Further activities

1. You could select a current news topic and ask all of the children to make their own conceptual art inspired by this topic, allowing each child to represent this concept in their own way.

Cross-curricular links

You could select a topic or concept from any curriculum area and ask the children to produce art inspired by it.

18 Gustav Klimt: Mixed media

In 30 seconds...

In these lessons, the children will learn about the history of the key artwork and explore key elements of Klimt's style. They will use photographic portraits of themselves to create a portrait inspired by the key artwork.

> ### Key artwork
>
> Gustav Klimt, *Adele Bloch-Bauer I*, oil, silver and gold on canvas, 1907

What do I need to know?

Gustav Klimt (1862–1918) was an Austrian painter who is now renowned as one of the great decorative painters of the twentieth century. In life, Klimt was a particularly private character and although he achieved fame in his lifetime, he avoided becoming the subject of gossip and divulged little about his home life. Klimt was born into a large family – he was one of seven siblings – and most members of the family had artistic tendencies, including his father who was a gold engraver originally from Bohemia, now the Czech Republic.

Klimt studied at the Vienna School of Arts and Crafts until 1883. In the early stages of his career as an artist, his style was classical and academically accurate; it did not yet have the decorative style of his later works. Klimt received commissions for murals and ceiling paintings, but in 1894 he painted a commission that the public and many others disliked and deemed to be inappropriate. Subsequently, Klimt never painted a public commission again.

Klimt was one of the founding members of the Vienna Secession. Unlike other groups of artists, the Secession did not have a defining style or release a manifesto. The group had commonalities with the English Arts and Crafts Movement and shared a belief that fine art and arts and crafts should be united. They also somewhat rejected the move towards machines and industrialisation and believed in the benefits to society of handmade objects.

Klimt's most well-known work comes from his 'golden phase', in which he used decorative patterns and gold leaf. The key artwork was a commission from his patrons, a wealthy Jewish couple, the Bloch-Bauers, and the portrait was to be a gift to Adele Bloch-Bauers' parents. Klimt made over two hundred studies of Adele Bloch-Bauer before beginning the painting, and the final piece is highly ornamental. It depicts Adele adorned with gold, shapes and symbols. The sitter's face, shoulders and hands are visible and are painted in a contrasting natural style. Adele looks both strong yet vulnerable in the pose. Critics claim that the work has Byzantine and Egyptian influences. During the Second World War, the Nazis confiscated the painting along with many other items from the homes of Jewish families. The painting was renamed *The Woman in Gold* so that it did not refer to a Jewish family. In the year 2000, the niece of Adele Bloch-Bauer successfully sued the Austrian government who had claimed ownership of the work after the war. She reclaimed the portrait along with other confiscated items. The 2015 film *Woman in Gold* tells this story.

- Klimt was an Austrian painter and is best known for his **decorative** style.
- Klimt's early work was considered **classical** in style and was vastly different to his more well-known pieces.
- Klimt's wealthy **patrons commissioned** him to paint the portrait of Adele Bloch-Bauer.
- The portrait includes gold leaf, shapes and symbols, and is highly **ornamental**.
- The painting was **confiscated** by the Nazis during the Second World War, and Adele Block-Bauer's niece later took the Austrian government to court to win the work back.

Vocabulary

Classical: Of an exemplary standard within a traditional and long-established style.
Commission: To order the production of something.
Confiscated: Take somebody's property with authority.
Decorative: Something made to look attractive.
Ornamental: Intended as decoration.
Patron: A person who gives support to an individual or organisation.

Useful links

www.gustav-klimt.com More information about Klimt and his works
www.theguardian.com/artanddesign/2011/feb/11/maria-altmann-obituary Obituary of Maria Altmann

Lesson 1 Composition

Key artwork
Gustav Klimt, *Adele Bloch-Bauer I*, oil, silver and gold on canvas, 1907

You will need
- A3 paper
- Photographs of the children, in the right proportions so as to have the head at the top of the A3 paper, in the same style as the key artwork
- Pencils
- Erasers
- Copies of the key artwork

Preparation
At some point before this lesson you will need to have taken and printed photographs of the class. It works best if the photographs are of the correct proportions so that when printed, the heads of the children can be cut and stuck onto A3 paper, in a similar style to the Klimt work. This can be done if you take a full-length photograph and then enlarge and print it onto A3 paper.

Getting started
Look at the key artwork and ask the children to comment on the artist's distinctive style, ask them to share how they would describe this work to someone, e.g. what are the defining features of the work? Encourage the children to notice the use of gold and the symbols and patterns in the work. Explain the history of the painting and discuss. Tell the children that this is one of Klimt's best-known works but many of his works were made in a similar style. Explain to the children that they will be making a self-portrait inspired by Klimt's work and that they will be using gold and Klimt's decorative style in addition to their own ideas. Their artwork should be original whilst also making visual links to Klimt.

Class activities
- Give the children their photograph and A3 paper, and allow them time to think about their composition, i.e. in which section of the paper they would like to cut and paste their head, allowing space for the surrounding decorations. The children may wish to replicate the position of Adele Bloch-Bauer or create a different composition.
- The children can then cut and stick their head onto their A3 paper.
- Let the children use their imagination and ideas from the Klimt image to decorate around the portrait, using light pencil marks first. They could include a cloak, robe or throne like the key artwork. They could even give the image a modern twist by including contemporary clothing.
- They should begin to include patterns and symbols like those they see in the Klimt image, as well as designing their own.

Plenary
Gather the children and look at their designs so far. Ask the children to comment on how their work is both similar and different to Klimt's. They could also talk a bit about their vision for the work and which colours they intend to use.

Lesson 2 Colour and pattern

Key artwork
Gustav Klimt, *Adele Bloch-Bauer I*, oil, silver and gold on canvas, 1907

You will need
- Children's work from the previous lesson
- Copies of the key artwork
- Pencils
- Erasers
- Black pens
- Watercolour paints
- Brushes
- Water pots
- Aprons

Preparation
Ensure that the children can access all the materials.

Getting started
Look at the key artwork and ask the children to comment on the colours used – highlight how the artist has predominantly used gold but has small areas of colour, including the lower part of the picture, which is green. Tell the children that they will be adding some areas of colour to their artwork in this lesson and they can also highlight patterns by using the pencil and black pen as the work develops. Explain that sometimes artists work with different materials at once and that sometimes ideas develop and change as the artist works.

Class activities
- Allow the children to work with a degree of freedom to develop their composition by adding pattern and colour.
- You may need to encourage children to step back from their work to ensure they do not over-develop the patterns and colour. It is useful to ask them to describe the specific parts that link to Klimt's work and then parts are their own ideas.
- Periodically remind the children that they can refer to the Klimt image for inspiration.

Plenary
Gather the children and look at their designs so far. Ask the children to comment on how their work is similar and how it is different to Klimt's. Explain that next lesson the children will have access to gold and ask them to think about how and where they will use it, refer to the key artwork for inspiration. You will see that the gold is layered in places and that there are shades of gold. Tell the children they will need to be selective about where they place the gold and they need to trust their artist's eyes about where it will look good.

Lesson 3 Gold

Key artwork
Gustav Klimt, *Adele Bloch-Bauer I*, oil, silver and gold on canvas, 1907

You will need
- Children's work from the previous lesson
- Copies of the key artwork
- Pencils
- Erasers
- Black pens
- Watercolour paints
- Brushes
- Water pots
- Gold glitter, pens and leaf
- PVA glue and spreaders
- Aprons

Preparation
Prepare the gold glitter in small containers so that the children can see that they have a limited amount to work with. Most gold leaf for schools will come in sheets, you will need to carefully cut the leaf into strips so that the children have access to a small amount each. If you wrap the leaf in tissue paper or tissue this should stop it flying away due to its light texture. This lesson involves a lot of materials and it is helpful if the children are able to access pens, paints, brushes and water independently; otherwise placing materials into a tray is a useful way of organising.

Getting started
Look at the key artwork and ask the children to comment on how the artist has used gold. Look at how it is layered, textured and drawn into. Explain that this lesson the children will add gold to their work and encourage them to add it in a way that makes visual links to the Klimt artwork. Remind the children that they may want to continue to develop other parts of their work, perhaps outlining patterns or adding sections of colour.

Class activities
- Allow the children to work with a degree of freedom to develop their composition by adding pattern, colour and gold.
- Encourage the children to step back and view their work to decide which parts of their composition needs working on or leaving alone. A helpful way to do this is in pairs, giving peer feedback.
- As you talk to the children, ask them to explain how they were influenced by Klimt and which ideas are their own, they should talk about specific parts of their work as well as the broader style links.

Plenary

Gather the children and look at their final pieces. You could select children to point out the pieces that are instantly recognisable as having links to Klimt and ask them to describe what the elements are that make that so. Encourage individual children to talk about their work and to explain why they made certain choices about composition or media. Ask the class to consider if they would make any changes to their work and explain that it is often a different experience making decisions whilst making work than it is looking at work once it is finished. You could end by posing the question, 'How does an artist know when they have finished?'.

Further activities

1. The children could make the portraits of each other as if fulfilling a commission like Klimt did.

Cross-curricular links

History: The children could study this painting at the same time as learning about the Second World War.

19 Michelle Reader: Figurative junk sculpture

In 30 seconds...

In these lessons, the children will look at the work of contemporary artist Michelle Reader. They will consider the human form and use recyclable materials to make a sculpture of an imaginary human.

Key artwork

Michelle Reader, *Seven Wasted Men*, scrap wood and household waste, 2006

What do I need to know?

The term 'figurative sculpture' conjures up images of grand marble sculptural work from Ancient Greece or Rome, however the earliest depictions of the human form in sculpture come from Europe around 25,000 years ago. Known as the *Venus figurines*, they are small sculptures that show exaggerated versions of the female form. Although their exact purpose remains unknown, they are thought to be associated with fertility.

The human body varies from person to person, but there are certainties around its proportions, and over the years, artists and anatomists have attempted to canonise the proportions for others to follow. Famously, Leonardo da Vinci's *Vitruvian Man* is a drawing in which the artist depicts the male figure based on the ideal human proportions. The drawing is inspired by the work of Vitruvius, a Roman architect, who believed that the geometry of the human body related to that of classical architecture. Da Vinci believed the workings of the human body to be reflective of the workings of the universe, and this drawing combines his own observations and ideas with rules set out by Vitruvius.

The medium and the technique used for figurative sculpture has often been influenced by the nature of the form being created and the range of materials available in the locality. Early sculptures were carved from stone and decorated with natural pigments, but today artists have any number of traditional and non-traditional materials available to them, as well as being at liberty to explore more abstract representations.

Michelle Reader is a contemporary artist who makes 'recycled sculptures from household and industrial waste combined with found objects sourced from charity shops and reclamation yards.' (Michelle Reader) Her work highlights environmental issues around human consumption and waste in a way that is accessible and easy to engage with. Michelle often uses found materials that help to tell the story of the subject, e.g. a postman made of junk mail.

On her website, Michelle Reader includes a description of the key artwork, *Seven Wasted Men*:

'These were commissioned by Cambridgeshire County Council in March 2006, as part of their Waste Reduction Campaign. They represent the fact that according to recent statistics we each produce seven times our own body weight each year in waste. Each one is created to the actual dimensions and with the physical characteristics of a real person, and Michelle used three weeks' worth of each person's own rubbish to make them.'

- The human form has long been a subject for **sculpture**.
- Early **figurative art** originates from Europe around 25,000 years ago, and the small sculptures of women are known as **Venus figurines**.
- Although human beings vary in shape and size, there are rules that artists follow to accurately depict the **proportions** of the human body.
- Michelle Reader makes art from junk and **recyclable** materials that might otherwise end up on a landfill. She transforms them to make figurative sculptures.
- Reader's work highlights **environmental issues** such as human consumption and waste.

Vocabulary

Environmental issues: Problems with the planet's systems that have developed because of human interference or mistreatment of the planet.
Figurative art: Any form of art that retains strong references to the real world, and particularly to the human figure.
Proportion: A part, share, or number considered in comparative relation to a whole.
Recyclable: A substance that can be recycled.
Sculpture: A three-dimensional representative or abstract form.
Venus figurines: A Stone Age statuette portraying women.

Useful links

www.michelle-reader.co.uk Michelle Reader's website
www.ancient-origins.net/ancient-places-europe/venus-figurines-european-paleolithic-era-001548 Information about the Venus figurines

Lesson 1 The human form

Key artwork
Michelle Reader, *Seven Wasted Men*, scrap wood and household waste, 2006

You will need
- Wooden mannequins, enough for each child to see one
- Pencils
- A3 paper, at least two sheets per child
- Erasers

Preparation
Fill an A3 piece of paper with sketches of the wooden mannequin in different poses; the sketches do not have to be of the whole mannequin, you could focus on particular parts.

Getting started
Explain to the children that artists have long been fascinated with the human form and that sculptures exist from the Stone Age that show this. Ask the children to recall how they used to draw humans when they were younger, e.g. stickmen, and explain that artists try to understand the basic proportions of the human form to help them to make sculptures of it. Show the children a wooden mannequin and explain that this is an artist's tool that is useful for making depictions of humans. Ask the children what they think make the mannequins useful, i.e. they do not have details but they show where there are joints in the body. Show the children how it is broken up into limbs, and how the limbs can be moved into different poses. Show the children your example, and tell them that they have to keep looking up at the mannequin to ensure that they draw from observation not memory.

Class activities
- Give the children wooden mannequins to look at and play with, and allow them to experiment with moving the mannequin into different poses.
- Encourage the children to understand how the mannequin corresponds to an actual human body.
- Ask the children to make several sketches of the mannequins in poses.

Plenary
Gather the children and look at their drawings, asking them to comment on challenges they came across. Explain that artists today use a variety of materials to make sculptures and are not limited to stone like the artists of the Stone Age. Show the children the key artwork by Michelle Reader and ask them to comment on the materials used. Explain why Reader uses these materials. Ask the children to collect materials from home to bring in and use for their sculptures next lesson.

Lesson 2 Junk modelling

Key artwork
Michelle Reader, *Seven Wasted Men*, scrap wood and household waste, 2006

You will need
- Wooden mannequins, enough for each child to see one
- The children's sketches from the previous lesson
- Junk and anything the children have brought in from home
- Masking tape
- PVA glue
- Glue spreaders
- Scissors

Preparation
Collect a variety of empty boxes and containers and ask the children to do the same, all contributing to a class collection of junk for making sculptures.

Getting started
Explain that the children will be working in groups to make a figurative junk model, look at some of the items with the children and ask them to suggest which body parts they could be used for. Look at the key artwork for inspiration and highlight the fact that the items that the children use can be varied and do not have to look exactly like the body part. Show the children how to use the masking tape or glue to join items together and explain that masking tape can be ripped by hand, which makes it easier to manipulate.

Class activities
- Allow the children to work in groups to create their sculptures, as large or small as you can accommodate but the bigger the better. Encourage the children to assist each other with joining items and to view their work from all angles.

Plenary
Have the children walk around and view each other's work, giving helpful suggestions and tips on techniques.

Lesson 3 Figurative junk sculptures

Key artwork
Michelle Reader, *Seven Wasted Men*, scrap wood and household waste, 2006

You will need
- Wooden mannequins, enough for each child to see one
- The children's sketches and the sculptures they started in the previous lesson

- Junk and anything the children have brought in from home
- Masking tape
- PVA glue
- Glue spreaders
- Scissors

Preparation
Ensure that the children have enough remaining packaging to use for their sculptures. If not, collect extra pieces.

Getting started
Remind the children that their sculpture should resemble the human form. Encourage them to look at their work so far alongside the mannequins, setting out targets for the lesson, e.g. include clearer knee joints.

Class activities
- Allow the children to work in their groups to finish creating their sculptures. Encourage the children to assist each other with joining items and to view their work from all angles.

Plenary
Have the children walk around and view each other's work. Ask the children to comment on the character of the figures that they have created. Ask the children to discuss challenges of working with recyclable materials and ask them to share any other ideas for reusing packaging.

Further activities

1. The children could make a sculpture for an area in the school – the piece could represent the ethos of the school or depict students.

Cross-curricular links

History: The children could make a sculpture of a famous historical figure.
Science: The children could look at Reader's work that incorporates moving parts and try to do the same in their sculptures.

20 William Morris: Designs with natural forms

In 30 seconds...

In these lessons, the children will look at the wallpaper designs of William Morris and they will learn about his approach to the decorative arts. The children will use their own natural form sketches and elements of Morris's designs to create a pattern.

Key artwork

William Morris, *Strawberry Thief*, block-printed cotton, 1883

What do I need to know?

William Morris (1834–1896) was an English artist, textile designer, writer, philosopher and social activist. Morris was a key part of the Arts and Crafts Movement which began in England and influenced North American and European culture. The movement advocated homemade and traditional crafts, a simple way of life and the decorative potential of everyday household items, especially poignant given the mechanisation of the Industrial Revolution. The Arts and Crafts Movement wanted a return to the dignified treatment of artists and craftspeople, as had been the case in the medieval era.

Morris was born into a wealthy family in Walthamstow in East London and went to the University of Oxford where he studied Classics. Morris married Jane Burden, who later became a favourite subject of the Pre-Raphaelite painters, and in 1860 they moved into a large house in Kent that was co-designed for them by friend and architect, Philip Webb. Morris and many of his artist friends decorated and completed the interior and garden of the house. It is known as the *Red House* and today it retains many of its original features and is open to the public. In 1861, encouraged by the success of the *Red House*, Morris and his Pre-Raphaelite friends founded a furnishings and decorative arts company, and they manufactured and sold handcrafted products.

The company, later known as the Firm, created a range of products, including stained glass, metalwork, furniture, embroidery and murals.

Around 1862, Morris began to focus on wallpaper designs, inspired to do so as he had experienced difficulties sourcing suitable paper when decorating his own home. Morris would observe flora and fauna first-hand in the gardens and hedgerows of England, and his patterns captured the beauty and rhythm of nature in an honest yet stylised way. Morris was always keen to learn all about production methods before designing, as he believed that the design process and production should not be far removed from each other, and where possible the artist should do it all. Morris's political views informed his artistic approach. He promoted an equal society and he was of the belief that art like education, for example, should be for all not for the few. Morris designed over fifty wallpapers and a specialist company chiselled the designs onto woodblocks and printed them using natural pigments as insisted on by Morris. The Firm underwent many changes and innovations in Morris's lifetime, and Morris continued to explore new enterprises as well as revive old techniques such as hand-knotted carpets. Morris & Co. is still a business today.

The Strawberry Thief pattern was inspired by thrushes that Morris saw in his garden and it was a design for textiles such as curtains, drapes or furniture covering.

- William Morris was part of the **Arts and Crafts Movement**.
- Morris and his friends advocated **handmade crafts**, traditional art forms and a return to the reverence of artists and craftspeople, as was the case in medieval times.
- Morris's beliefs considering the **Industrial Revolution** were poignant.
- Morris and his friends established a successful **decorative arts** company.
- Morris began to focus on designs for wallpaper **patterns** and these are what he is most well-known for today.
- Morris insisted on understanding the **production** of his designs as well as the use of **natural pigments**.
- Morris took his inspiration from the **direct observation** of nature found in his local area.

Vocabulary

Arts and Crafts Movement: A movement in the decorative and fine arts that began in Britain and spread to Europe and North America between 1880 and 1910.
Decorative arts: Art and crafts produced for both aesthetic value and functionality.
Direct observation: Collecting information by watching the subject at first hand.
Handmade crafts: Made by hand, not by machine.
Industrial Revolution: The development of industry that occurred in the late eighteenth and nineteenth centuries, brought about by the introduction of machinery.
Natural pigment: An organically found substance that gives something a colour when it is added to it, such as in plants, flowers and fruits.
Pattern: A repeated design.
Production: The process of making something from raw materials.

Useful links

www.collections.vam.ac.uk/item/O78889/strawberry-thief-furnishing-fabric-morris-william Image of the *Strawberry Thief*
www.william-morris.co.uk A company that sells Morris designs

Lesson 1 Observational drawing

Key artwork
William Morris, *Strawberry Thief*, block-printed cotton, 1883

You will need
- A collection of natural forms, e.g. pine cones, shells and flowers
- Pencils
- Erasers
- A3 paper folded into approximately eight sections
- Examples of Morris's designs in handout form
- Tracing paper in squares, approximately 10cm x 10cm – one for you to demonstrate with

Preparation
Lay out the natural forms so that the children can select and sketch a range easily. Find a range of examples of Morris's designs and print in A4 format.

Getting started
Show the children the key artwork and ask them to share what they can see in the artwork, e.g. birds and plants, and ask them to say what they notice about the style of this artwork, e.g. that it has repeated patterns and it has symmetry. Ask the children to discuss whether they think this is the kind of art that you would see on a wall and if not, where do they think they would see art with patterns and symmetry. Explain that the artwork is a design for fabric and tell the children some information about Morris, his work and his ideals. Explain that Morris was often inspired by natural forms and this is evident in his designs for wallpaper and textiles. Ensure that the children understand how the Arts and Crafts Movement was set against the backdrop of industrialisation and contrasted with it. Explain that like Morris, the children will be developing their own design for a textile of wallpaper pattern. Tell them they will be using natural forms as inspiration and combining them with Morris's designs to create their work. Tell the children that they will begin by making sketches of natural forms, these will later be developed into a design.

Class activities
- Ask the children to fold their A3 paper into eight sections and demonstrate how they how they can fill each section of their paper with a different sketch of a natural form.
- They do not have to sketch the whole object but can focus on lines and shapes that they like, e.g. a spiral on a shell or the wavy patterns on a pine cone.
- Ask the children to make sketches of some of the natural forms in each of the sections on their paper; they should try to fill each section and they do not need to include shading.

Plenary
Gather the children and look at their drawings of natural forms, explain that next week they will be combining their designs with parts of Morris's designs to create a new design. Show the children the square of tracing paper and ask them to feedback on what is and what it is used for. Demonstrate how you can search through the Morris designs, selecting parts to trace such as the bird from the key artwork. Then show how you can trace the bird with a dark pencil outline onto your square of tracing paper. Show how you can then use the same piece of tracing paper to trace a section of one of the children's observational drawings; you are combining the two to create a whole new design. You can trace as many different parts of designs from Morris

and the natural form sketches as you like, until you are happy with the composition on the square of tracing paper. It is best to keep the lines and shapes clear and relatively simple as you be retracing over these lines several times.

Lesson 2 Design creation

Key artwork
William Morris, *Strawberry Thief*, block-printed cotton, 1883

You will need
- The children's designs from the previous lesson
- Pencils
- Erasers
- Examples of Morris's designs in handout form
- Tracing paper in squares, approximately 10cm x 10cm – one each, plus extra for any mistakes
- A4 paper

Preparation
Create your own design on a tracing paper square. To do this, trace elements from one of the children's observational drawings and combine it with your favourite parts of Morris's designs as in the demonstration in last lessons plenary. Be careful to select clear shapes rather than parts which include intricate details.

Getting started
Show the children your example of a design on the tracing paper. Recap how, by using the tracing paper, you could select parts of the observational drawings the children produced last lesson, and combine them with your favourite parts of the William Morris designs. Demonstrate to the children how they can rotate the tracing paper to build an interesting design and even repeat details that they like, e.g. a curved line from a shell could appear on every corner of the tracing paper square.

Class activities
- Give the children their square of tracing paper and encourage them to have a good look at their sketches and the Morris designs before tracing.
- Let the children begin their design. Encourage them to select clear shapes rather than intricate details. The designs should not be too 'busy'.
- They should apply pressure to pencil as they trace them.

Plenary
Gather the children and look at their traced designs. Explain that the next step is to create the repeat pattern onto A4 paper. Tell the children that the tracing paper can be used to do this, using a method called trace and transfer. This is because the pencil marks are easily transferred from the tracing paper to the A4 paper.

Demonstrate to the children how to place the square of tracing paper with the design on it in the top corner of the A4 paper. Holding the tracing paper still, you can then retrace the design; it is important that the original pencil design is touching the paper so that you are retracing over the back of the original pencil mark. This will cause the original pencil marks to imprint on to the A4 sheet underneath. This method will transfer the design from the tracing paper onto the plain paper. You must apply pressure to ensure transference and be sure that the tracing paper is pencil-side-down on the plain paper because the pencil drawing needs to touch the paper to transfer onto it.

Show the children how you can flip the design over and create a repeat pattern by retracing the design again and again, placing the tracing paper right next to the first transfer to create an interconnected pattern. The transfer might appear light on the paper and you may need to draw over it again with your pencil. It may only be possible to create two or three rows of the repeat pattern before the tracing paper gets too smudged.

Lesson 3 Transfer pattern

Key artwork
William Morris, *Strawberry Thief*, block-printed cotton, 1883

You will need
- The children's designs on tracing paper from the previous lesson
- Pencils
- Erasers
- A4 paper, one sheet each

Preparation
Create your own pattern by tracing and transferring your design in rows and columns onto a sheet of A4 paper.

Getting started
Remind the children how to trace and transfer, ensuring that they know that they must have the pencil side of the tracing paper touching the A4 paper to transfer. Tell the children to try and line the tracing paper up as close as possible to the previous transfer to create their pattern. Repeat that they must apply pressure to the pencil to transfer, and that they might have to go over the pencil mark freehand, to make it stand out.

Class activities
- Give the children their A4 paper and allow them to begin the trace and transfer technique.
- The children should try to complete at least two rows to see a pattern emerge.

Plenary
Gather the children and look at their patterns. Discuss whether they can imagine them being developed into a wallpaper design. Read or show the children the quote by William Morris (1880): 'Have nothing in your house that you do not know to be useful, or believe to be beautiful.' Have them discuss how this relates to their idea of the home and art.

Further activities

1. The children could develop their patterns further by making print tiles from them using lino, foam or polystyrene.
2. They could extend the pencil patterns by mixing and painting their own colours.

Cross-curricular links

Maths: Make links to symmetry, repeating patterns and rotational patterns.
History: You could teach this alongside a scheme about the Industrial Revolution.

21 Willem Kalf: Still life painting

In 30 seconds...

In these lessons, the children will learn about still life painting through the study of the key artwork by Willem Kalf. They will come to understand his choice of objects in the key artwork as well as learning about composition and watercolour painting techniques. They will create their own still life compositions and a layered watercolour painting.

Key artwork

Willem Kalf, *Still life with Drinking Horn*, oil on canvas, c.1653 (see Figure 21A, and 21B and 21C for children's work)

What do I need to know?

Still life painting as a genre is evident in the ancient world but it does not have a strong presence in art history again until the sixteenth century. In the early sixteenth century, northern Europe was a centre for still life painting, due in large part to a decline in religious paintings because of the Protestant revolt against the Roman Catholic church. The production of oil paints as a medium also had a part to play, as the slow drying time allowed painters to rework pieces, leading to more detailed and therefore impressive artworks. The still life genre has continued to draw the attention of artists, and while the style and approach may differ, often the objects remain of a similar type, e.g. flowers, fruits, vases, fabric, etc. Although the depiction of inanimate objects may seem uninteresting, the artist makes a deliberate selection based on the qualities of form, texture, colour, etc. and arranges them in an interesting composition to offset and highlight these qualities – in some cases the objects also hold a symbolic meaning.

Willem Kalf (1619–1693) was a Dutch still life painter. His most well-known works are in the 'Pronkstilleven' style, which translates as 'ostentatious still life', in which artists painted objects to depict the opulence and abundance of seventeenth century Holland. Kalf's paintings were highly sought after by the affluent in Amsterdam and the contents of his paintings give us an insight into what life was like for them. The objects chosen often held meaning and were read as symbols. Works of art that include motifs alluding to the transience of life and the unimportance of worldly goods are known as 'Vanitas'. Some critics believe that the Vanitas genre was used as justification for painting luxurious objects.

The key artwork displays Kalf's talent for painting surfaces, textures and light. It shows a collection of expensive objects that celebrate the pleasures experienced by the wealthy in Amsterdam. At the time, the city was one of the largest and most thriving in Europe; it was a centre for international trade. The wealth in the city meant that individuals could afford to be patrons of art and commission paintings. The key artwork painting features a drinking horn, which belonged to the Saint Sebastian Archer's guild, a group of archers tasked with protecting the town from attack. It is likely that they commissioned the painting. On special occasions, the group would meet for feasts, and the horn would be filled with wine and passed around the table.

Since Amsterdam was a centre for trade, many exotic goods were available to those that could afford them. The carpet in the painting was likely to have been imported from Persia – it was often the custom to place valuable carpets on the table rather than the floor. The glass to the right of the painting is probably made from Venetian glass as it is cut in a typically Venetian style, and the lemon was possibly imported from warmer climes, although it could have been grown in a Dutch hothouse. Although seafood would have been readily available, a lobster would have been more expensive than most.

The composition is set in front of an extremely dark background and the red of the lobster is vibrant against it. The centre of the painting is the lobster's eye and Kalf has expertly depicted the surface of the shell. The lemon is shown semi-peeled and could be seen a symbol of the bitterness of life as well as being placed in opposition to the sweetness of the wine next to it.

- **Still life** painting in the seventeenth century was a flourishing genre in the Netherlands.
- Still life paintings depict **inanimate objects**.
- The key artwork depicts many objects associated with **opulence** and luxury.
- The **composition** is set against a dark background that highlights the brightness of the red lobster.
- The objects in the still life would have been familiar to the wealthy of Amsterdam at the time.
- Amsterdam was a flourishing city and many **exotic** items were **imported**.
- Kalf was a master at depicting **textures**, surfaces and light.

Vocabulary

Composition: Combining parts to make a whole.
Exotic: Originating from a foreign country.
Imported: Brought from another country to sell.
Inanimate objects: Lacking the power of motion or consciousness.
Opulence: Lavishness or wealth.
Still life: A genre of art typically depicting inanimate objects on a surface.
Texture: The feel or perceived feel of a surface.

Useful links

www.nationalgallery.org.uk/paintings/willem-kalf-still-life-with-drinking-horn *Still life with drinking horn*
www.tate.org.uk/learn/online-resources/glossary/s/still-life Information about still life

Lesson 1 Composition

Key artwork
Willem Kalf, *Still life with Drinking Horn*, oil on canvas, c.1653

You will need
- Whiteboards and pens, one each
- A collection of still life objects (see Preparation)

Preparation
Collect a range of still life objects: these should vary in height and shape and there should be enough for pairs or a small table of children to see at least three objects – you could opt for more traditional items such as vases, bottles, fruits, shells, fabric, or you could collect contemporary items to represent the children's lives.

Getting started
Show the children the key artwork and ask them to share and discuss the items that they can see. Ask whether the children can identify any links between the items and if they know what style of painting this is known as. Explain that it is a still life. Tell the children about the history of still life painting and describe its popularity in the seventeenth century. Discuss Kalf's choice of objects and ask the children to consider what items they would include if they were to try and say something about their lives, e.g. iPads, pencil cases, etc. Talk with the children about the composition and explain that when an artist paints a still life, they try to make an interesting composition first, like in Kalf's painting.

Class activities
- Give the children access to still life objects and allow them some time to work in pairs or groups to arrange the items into a composition.
- Prompt the children by giving them pointers about not having the objects too far apart and having a mixture of heights.
- Ask the children to view their composition from the seat they will be drawing from, making sure that the composition works well for everyone.
- Bring the children's attention back to the key artwork and point out how the items sometimes overlap and explain that it can be tricky to draw objects behind or in front of each other (children tend to spread the objects out in their drawing, not drawing what they see).
- Demonstrate this by drawing two overlapping circles on a whiteboard. Erase one of the overlapping lines to create the effect that one of the circles is in front of the other. Then redraw that line and erase the other overlapping line, to create the effect that the other circle is now in front.
- Ask the children to practise drawing their compositions on their whiteboards, breaking down the objects into manageable shapes and then adding details of the shapes.
- Encourage the children to draw the objects that overlap, e.g. draw things as they see them, from observation not imagination or memory.

Plenary

Gather the children and ask them to discuss any challenges they came across when drawing from direct observation. Explain that in the next lesson they will be drawing with a pencil and will have to press down really softly so that they can easily erase lines if they need to.

Lesson 2 Colour wash

Key artwork
Willem Kalf, *Still life with Drinking Horn*, oil on canvas, c.1653

You will need
- A4 watercolour paper or thick cartridge paper
- Pencils
- Watercolour paints
- Medium brushes
- Water pots
- Still life objects from last lesson
- Pieces of board to create the still life compositions on or a camera to photograph them to remember for next lesson

Preparation
Have the watercolour paints and water pots easily accessible for the second part of the lesson. Have the children make their compositions on pieces of board or take photographs of the setups so that you can recreate them for next lesson.

Getting started
Remind the children how to set up a composition and give them a few minutes to do this on their tables or in pairs, making sure that each child has a good view of the objects. Explain to the children that they will be sketching the composition and remind them to draw from observation – the drawing does not need to have any detail; it should be a quick line drawing (see Figure 21B for children's work).

Class activities
- Give the children a short amount of time only to lightly sketch their compositions, to stop them adding too much detail. Ensure they have filled their paper – it is preferable for the drawing to go over the edges of the page rather than be too small in the centre of the paper.
- Show the children how to make the watercolour paints watery and paint broad patches of colour to match the main colours of the still life. This should not be with any detail and the children should not add dark shades or shadows at this stage – this is a watercolour wash.
- Next the children can start to layer areas of slightly darker shades but still with no detail and no black.

Plenary

Gather the children to look at their work so far. Ask them to comment on each other's compositions. Explain that next lesson the children will continue to layer the colours, adding some areas of detail and trying to show the textures of the objects.

Lesson 3 Textures and details

Key artwork

Willem Kalf, *Still life with Drinking Horn*, oil on canvas, c.1653

You will need

- The children's paintings from last lesson
- Still life objects from last lesson set up as before
- Watercolour paints
- Medium and thin brushes
- Water pots
- Tissues for dabbing brushes
- Aprons

Preparation

Have the watercolour paints and water pots easily accessible for all the children. Set the still life compositions up in the same place as previous lesson and ensure the children sit in the same spaces.

Getting started

Remind the children that they have completed a line drawing and a colour wash so far, and tell them that now they can add darker shades and details of the items. Bring the children's attention to Kalf's work and how he showed details and textures. Ask the children to sit and look at their compositions before painting them. Ask them to notice the details and textures on the objects and invite them to share some words that describe the textures they can see.

Class activities

- Let the children continue to add colour to their work – remind them how to make tints and shades by adding white or black to the original colour.
- Encourage the children to use different brushstrokes to create the impression of different textures.
- Remind the children to include the shadows, using dark blue rather than black for these.
- Children can use the thin brushes to add details.

Plenary

Gather the children and review the still life process from setting up the composition to the completed artwork. Ask the children to comment on how successful they think each other's work is and why.

Further activities

1. The children could have an extra lesson to add the finer details with a thin brush.

Cross-curricular links

History: The children could look at examples of still life murals from the ancient world, e.g. from Pompeii.

22 Maria Sibylla Merian: Scientific illustration

In 30 seconds...

In these lessons, the children will learn about the artist Maria Sibylla Merian and her illustrations, as well as her dedication to studying and recording nature. They will create their own life cycle illustrations, with detail and consideration of aesthetic value.

Key artwork

Maria Sibylla Merian, *Cotton-Leaf Physicnut with Giant Sphinx Moth*, watercolour and bodycolour with gum arabic over lightly etched outlines on vellum, 1702–1703

What do I need to know?

Early Medieval illustrations were hand painted and restricted to one-offs, but around 1455, the invention of the printer changed Western civilisation: the printed book could reach a wider audience and illustrations could be reproduced to accompany the text. Before the age of modern technology, illustrated books were the only source of visual information about animals, plants, different species and places as reported on by explorers and scientists of the time. Illustrations would have been the only way for curious members of the public to see new discoveries and learn about the world beyond what they had seen with their own eyes. In the seventeenth and eighteenth century, Merian produced and published watercolour paintings and engravings of plants, animals and perhaps most memorably, insects.

Maria Sibylla Merian (1647–1717) was a German naturalist, entomologist, botanical artist and scientific illustrator. Her work has appeal for science and art lovers alike. Merian achieved much in her lifetime that was unthinkable for a woman of that period, and her contributions to biology are steadily being recognised as a significant part of scientific history.

Born in Germany to a wealthy family, Merian would copy illustrations of flowers from the books available to her at home – her father owned a publishing house. At thirteen years of age, Merian, apparently dissatisfied with copying from books, began raising and observing silkworms, sparking a lifelong interest. Merian was soon branching out to collect, observe and record caterpillars, pupae, butterflies, and moths. She was a talented artist and accurately depicted the creatures at various stages of their life cycles, making notes in German to complement her findings.

Merian's first book in 1675 focused on botanical illustrations, but she was particularly fascinated by the process of metamorphosis, which at that time was not fully understood. In 1679, she published her first book on entomology. In this book, Merian's illustrations were a first in that they depicted insects at different stages of their life cycles and in their habitat, all within one image.

In 1699, aged 52, Merian made a radical decision for the times and left her husband to pursue her passion for collecting and depicting strange types of flora, fauna, animals and insects. She and her daughter travelled to Suriname in South America. Merian raised funds by selling her work and she also received a grant from the city of Amsterdam where she had been studying specimens – a first for a woman. In Suriname, the landscape was very different to that of the gardens that Merian had been used to; it is hard to imagine her and her daughter in petticoats and corsets exploring the South American jungle – it was a brave adventure to undertake for anyone, let alone a woman of that era. It is after this trip that Merian published her most well-known book, *Metamorphosis Insectorum Surinamensium*. The book is full of illustrations of the tropical species of Suriname, many unknown in Europe at the time. The images are in Merian's typical style; she shows the connections between related organisms in an 'ecological' composition that often includes food and habitat. Before Merian, these would have been separate images, but she set a new standard.

- Before the printer was invented around 1455, early Medieval **illustrations** were hand painted one-offs – books were the privilege of the wealthy.
- Before the development of technology such as photography and the Internet, illustrated books were the only format for passing on visual information.
- Maria Siyblla Merian was an **entomologist**, **naturalist**, **botanical artist** and **scientific illustrator**.
- Merian's work is increasingly valued for its contributions to scientific history as well as her illustrations being objects of artistic value.
- Merian was fascinated by the subject of **metamorphosis** – which was not fully understood at the time.
- Merian's illustrations were the first to depict the holistic **life cycle** of a creature, often including significant elements of the habitat and food of the subject, all in a single composition.
- Merian made a brave expedition to Suriname in South America and produced extensive illustrations and notes on tropical species there.

Vocabulary

Botanical artist: The art of depicting the plant species in a scientifically accurate way.
Entomologist: A person who studies insects.
Illustration: Pictures that accompany text, intended for further explanation, clarification or adornment.
Life cycle: The series of changes in the life of an organism.
Metamorphosis: The process of transforming from an immature form to an adult form in distinct stages.
Naturalist: A person who studies natural history.
Scientific illustrator: Artists in the service of science for which accuracy and communication are essential.

Useful links

www.royalcollection.org.uk/collection/921195/cotton-leaf-physicnut-with-giant-sphinx-moth *Cotton-Leaf Physicnut with Giant Sphinx Moth*
www.botanicalartandartists.com/about-maria-sibylla-merian.html Artist information

Lesson 1 Specialist species

Key artwork
Maria Sibylla Merian, *Cotton-Leaf Physicnut with Giant Sphinx Moth*, watercolour and bodycolour with gum arabic over lightly etched outlines on vellum, 1702–1703

You will need
- Access to the Internet and printing capability for each child
- Pencils
- Erasers
- A3 paper

Preparation
The children will need access to computers and a printer for research into lifecycles of animals. It may be useful to find a few useful websites for this, to advise the children.

Getting started
Show the children the key artwork and ask them to share what they learn from looking at the image; what do they think the artist was trying to achieve in this work? Explain the context of the work and ask the children to imagine life without today's easy access to information. Highlight how the work depicts the whole life cycle of the insect and includes the plant that the moth feeds on. Ensure that the children have access to the Internet and explain that they are going to be scientific illustrators. Ask them to select one living organism to illustrate and give them the chance to research online.

Class activities
- Encourage the children to print out images of their chosen subject at different stages of its life cycle.
- The children should also make notes and sketches on their paper.
- The children could begin to plan their composition, ensuring that they include visual information about the various stages of the subject's life.

Plenary
Gather the children and ask them to share some information about their subject.

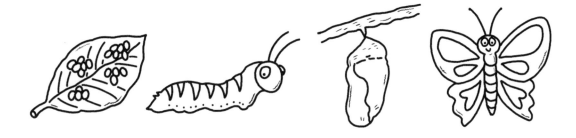

Lesson 2 Composition

Key artwork
Maria Sibylla Merian, *Cotton-Leaf Physicnut with Giant Sphinx Moth*, watercolour and bodycolour with gum arabic over lightly etched outlines on vellum, 1702–1703

You will need
- Children's research from the previous lesson
- Pencils
- Erasers
- A3 paper or watercolour paper, one each
- Watercolour paints
- Brushes in various sizes
- Aprons

Preparation
Set the equipment out so that each child has access.

Getting started
Show the children the key artwork again and highlight how the artist has included the insect at several stages of its life, e.g. as a caterpillar, in a cocoon, as a moth. Explain that they now need to sketch their own compositions in a similar style, using their research from the previous lesson.

Class activities
- The children should now sketch out their chosen subject, making sure they include the different stages of its life cycle.
- If they complete this, they can begin to add colour but save adding details for the next lesson.

Plenary
Gather the children and ask them to share their work so far. Encourage them to question each other about the work so far so that they each get an idea of how informative their compositions are.

Lesson 3 Scientific illustration

Key artwork
Maria Sibylla Merian, *Cotton-Leaf Physicnut with Giant Sphinx Moth*, watercolour and bodycolour with gum arabic over lightly etched outlines on vellum, 1702–1703

You will need
- Children's research from the previous lesson
- Pencils
- Erasers
- A3 paper or watercolour paper
- Watercolour paints
- Brushes in various sizes
- Aprons

Preparation
Set the equipment out so that each child has access.

Getting started
Look at the children's artwork from last lesson, and recap that their composition must enable the viewer to learn something about the chosen species, just by looking at the illustration. Allow the children to consider their targets for the lesson to achieve this goal. Show the children how to use the thin brush like a pencil to add details.

Class activities
- The children should now continue to develop their work, using a thin brush to add any details.

Plenary
Have a gallery walk: display the children's work and all walk around to look at them. Ask the children to imagine that these illustrations were their only source of visual information about these subjects, and ask them to give feedback about what they have learnt from the scientific illustrations.

Further activities

1. The children could carry out this research and illustration work following a residential trip or a day trip to a zoo, aquarium or botanical gardens. They could present the illustrations to another year group to ascertain their usefulness as scientific illustrations.

Cross-curricular links

History: Merian could be studied as part of a programme of study on significant females through history.
Science: There are obvious links to be made with a science topic on living things.

23 Henry Moore: Family unit sculptures

In 30 seconds...

In these lessons, the children will learn about the artist Henry Moore and his sculpture work on family units. They will consider ways of representing their own family unit and make a small clay sculpture of it.

> ### Key artwork
>
> Henry Moore, *Family Group*, bronze, 1949

What do I need to know?

Henry Spencer Moore (1898–1986) was an English sculptor and artist, who achieved many prestigious commendations for his contributions to the art world during his lifetime. Moore is probably best known for his huge semi-abstract sculptures depicting reclining figures and family groups. Moore's sculptures can be seen in many public spaces around the world, and in Hertfordshire, the public can visit the Henry Moore Foundation.

Moore's childhood was spent in Yorkshire. His father was a miner who nurtured other interests such as Shakespeare and playing the violin. The family would take walks in the Yorkshire landscape and Moore often referred to these times as influential to his work. It is said that Moore was inspired to be a sculptor after hearing a story about Michelangelo at Sunday school. Moore showed early promise as an artist but was persuaded by his parents to train as a teacher. At the age of eighteen, Moore enrolled in the army and he served in the First World War, enduring an injury in 1917. Moore convalesced and after the war he received a grant, which he used to study art in Leeds. After a few years' study in drawing, Moore finally embarked on a sculpture course and was the only full-time sculpture student at Leeds School of Art.

In around 1921, Moore moved to London to study sculpture at the Royal Academy. Subsequently, Moore had stints teaching at the Royal Academy and Chelsea school of Art as well as working on his own art; he was already a well-respected artist. In 1940, during the Second World War, Moore and his wife moved out of their home in London due to bomb damage – they moved to Herefordshire and although they had intended to return to London, the couple stayed for the rest of their lives and their house now forms part of the Henry Moore Foundation sculpture gardens. During the war, Moore was asked by an official government body to take the role of official Second World War artist. Moore observed and drew people in underground bomb shelters.

Moore took inspiration from nature and natural forms such as bones and shells. His sculptures often make visual links to these forms and his work was mostly intended to be placed and viewed in public places. After the war, many of Moore's family sculptures became a symbol of optimism, and the key artwork is one of these well-known post-war bronzes. Moore began planning this sculpture and had two sketchbooks full of preparatory sketches; he was trying to create a piece that would hold appeal to adults and children – the sculpture was commissioned for the grounds of a new school which was going to be the centre of a community. The sculpture shows a family unit and the parents are enveloping their small child, with their arms forming a kind of secure knot. Moore continued his sculpture plans by developing his drawings into maquettes and although the initial school was not able to fund the final stages of production, Moore was commissioned to complete the work by another school.

- Henry Moore is a well-loved British artist and **sculptor**, renowned for his **semi-abstract** figurative sculptures.
- Moore's sculptures can be seen in public spaces around the world.
- Moore lived through two world wars and during the Second World War he was the official artist, recording people sheltering in underground tube tunnels as bomb shelters.
- Moore was inspired by natural forms and landscapes.
- After the Second World War, Moore's family sculptures became synonymous with post-war optimism.
- The key artwork was a commission for a new school. It showed a **conventional family unit**.
- Moore created preparatory sketches and a **maquette** before making the final bronze piece.

Vocabulary

Conventional: In accordance with what is generally done.
Family unit: A basic social unit consisting of parents and their children.
Maquette: A small preliminary model or sketch.
Sculptor: An artist who makes sculptures.
Semi-abstract: The subject remains recognisable although the forms may be stylised.

Useful links

www.tate.org.uk/art/research-publications/henry-moore/henry-moore-om-ch-family-group-r1172198 *Family group*
www.henry-moore.org Artist foundation website

Lesson 1 Preliminary sketches

Key artwork
Henry Moore, *Family Group*, bronze, 1949

You will need
- A4 Paper, one each
- Pencils or charcoal

- Erasers
- Wooden mannequins
- Air-dry clay

Preparation
Make your own sketch of a family group using abstract figures.

Getting started
Look at the key artwork and ask the children to discuss what they can see. Explain that after the Second World War, sculptures like these were important to promote a more optimistic outlook. Ask the children to discuss why this sculpture might be comforting. Explain a bit about the context of the work and explain that this lesson the children will be creating some preparatory sketches for their own sculpture, for which they will then use clay to make a maquette.

Class activities
- Ask the children to think about their own families or the people that live with them in their houses.
- The children can then make some sketches of their ideas for their own family group sculpture, keeping in mind that the figures can be semi-abstract.
- The children can use the wooden mannequins to help them to work out how to draw the figures.
- Show the children your example.
- If the children used charcoal, spray the work with fixative or hairspray to stop smudging. Do not do this while the children are in the classroom.

Plenary
Gather the children and use one of their designs as a guide to show the children how they can take a small piece of air-dry clay and sculpt it into a maquette. Explain that this is what they will be doing next lesson.

Lesson 2 Building a maquette

Key artwork
Henry Moore, *Family Group*, bronze, 1949

You will need
- Children's drawings from last lesson
- Wooden mannequins
- Air-dry clay
- Cling film

Preparation
Use your drawing and develop it into a small clay maquette.

Getting started

Look again at the key artwork and draw the children's attention to how the figures have no details on the faces and the way the figures are simplified and curvy. Explain that this lesson the children be making their maquettes and will need to make sure that they check their sculptures from all angles. Show the children your example.

Class activities

- Give the children a small piece of clay and allow them to sculpt their pieces.
- The children will need to wrap the unfinished maquettes in cling film to keep them from drying out before the next lesson.

Plenary

Gather the children with their sculptures and discuss any challenges they have had using the clay. Ask the children to comment on their sculptures, describing their family units.

Lesson 3 Family group sculptures

Key artwork

Henry Moore, *Family Group*, bronze, 1949

You will need

- Children's drawings and clay sculptures from the last two lessons
- Air-dry clay
- Wooden mannequins

Preparation

Add any additional parts to your example.

Getting started

Review the children's work from last lesson and ask the children to consider what they need to do in this lesson to complete their maquettes.

Class activities

- Allow the children time to complete their work, ensuring that the sculpture is three-dimensional.

Plenary

Gather the children with their sculptures and ask them to give feedback to each other. Ask the children to try and envisage their sculptures in a public space, and ask them where they think that would be.

Further activities

1. Instead of making figurative sculptures, the children could design a different work of art that they think could uplift the public.

Cross-curricular links

History: Studies of Henry Moore could work well alongside studies of the Second World War – for this you could introduce the children to Moore's drawings of people sheltering in the underground tube tunnels.

24 Elizabeth Catlett: Printing portraits

In 30 seconds...

In these lessons, the children will learn about the ethos of the artist Elizabeth Catlett, and they will consider the individuals that they meet in their day-to-day lives as subjects for art. The children will create a print of and possibly for an individual that may not otherwise have time to appreciate art.

Key artwork

Elizabeth Catlett, *Sharecropper*, linoleum cut, 1952

What do I need to know?

Elizabeth Catlett (1915–2012) was an American sculptor, painter and printmaker. She used her art to advance issues that were important to her, particularly the Civil Rights Movement and the plight of everyday hard-working individuals. Catlett believed that art should be for the benefit of all people and not the preserve of the elite.

Catlett was the granddaughter of freed slaves, and her grandmother would share stories of the struggles of plantation life. She was born in Washington DC and was brought up by her mother as her father had died before she was born. Her mother was supportive of her artistic leniencies and Catlett records having made a soap sculpture of an elephant in high school. She graduated in art and design in 1936 and went on to study and master various other disciplines, including sculpture and printmaking. As well as her own studies, she held various teaching jobs, most rewarding of which was as an adult education teacher where she felt she was fulfilling her passion of 'working for the people'. She continued to gain notoriety and had well-received exhibitions in America. In 1962, Catlett relocated to Mexico and found it an inspirational climate for producing her art. While in Mexico she produced a series of linocuts depicting black, female labourers, artists and farmers.

Because of her ethos when it came to art appreciation, Catlett formed an affiliation with Mexico and Mexican artists such as muralist Diego Rivera, who also made art that made political statements. Working with a mainly black subject matter, Catlett produced work to 'be of service to black people' and to represent and relate to a black audience. She recognised that everyday working class people may not have the leisure time or money to engage with high art or formally study art, and she was trying to raise artistic appreciation and engage such people.

From the 1960s through to the 1980s, Catlett received many awards and commissions in both the United States and Mexico, and she continued to uphold her approach of making art that everyday people could relate to and understand in an intuitive way.

After the abolition of slavery and the civil war, the American South was unstable; many of the plantations were ceased by the government to be later returned to landowners who found themselves without a workforce. The freedmen were offered sharecropping as a means to produce crops and earn a living, a system whereby the landowner took a portion of the crops produced in exchange for the cropper working a plot of their land. The key artwork depicts a sharecropper looking dignified and holding her head high.

- Catlett was an artist who used her art to advance the issues that she felt strongly about, such as the **Civil Rights Movement**.
- Catlett's grandmother was a freed slave and would tell her stories of the struggles of **plantation** life.
- Catlett found that she had much in common with Mexican **mural** artists such as Diego Rivera, and she eventually moved to Mexico.
- Catlett was dedicated to creating art that could be appreciated and understood by ordinary people, even if they had no formal training in art appreciation.
- The key artwork is a **linoleum cut** and there are a few versions, some with colour on the face of the woman.
- The woman in the artwork is a sharecropper.

Vocabulary

Civil Rights Movement: A struggle by African Americans in the mid 1950s to late 1960s to achieve civil rights equal to those of white people.
Linoleum cut: A printmaking technique, a variant of woodcut, in which a sheet of linoleum is cut into.
Mural: A large painting made on or fixed to a wall.
Plantation: A farm or estate, usually in a tropical country, in which crops such as cotton, tobacco, coffee, sugar, etc. is cultivated, historically by African slaves.

Useful links

www.moma.org/collection/works/88189?locale=en *Sharecropper*
www.nmwa.org/explore/artist-profiles/elizabeth-catlett Artist information

---

Lesson 1 An everyday subject

Key artwork
Elizabeth Catlett, *Sharecropper*, linoleum cut, 1952

You will need
- Images of individuals that the children may encounter every day, e.g. teachers, cashiers, bus drivers, waiting staff, caretaker, etc.
- A4 Paper, one each

- Pencils
- Erasers
- Foam tiles (or lino) one each

Preparation
Find and print images of individuals that the children may encounter every day, e.g. teachers, cashiers, bus drivers, waiting staff, caretaker, etc. There needs to be enough for children to share or have one each.

Getting started
Look at the key artwork and ask the children to comment on who they think the lady might be. Explain that the artwork is a print and encourage the children to notice the different types of lines that the artist has used. Remind them how the printing process works and that the white areas would be the areas that had been cut away. Explain a bit more about Catlett's ethos and motivations for producing art and ask the children to reflect on whether they know anyone who may not have the time or inclination to appreciate art – this could be someone that they know well or not; it could be someone they perceive to be busy and hardworking.

Class activities
- Give the children some paper and ask them to sketch a line drawing portrait of the person they have in mind; the person might be wearing an item of clothing that makes them identifiable, such as a uniform of some sort.
- Ask the children to fill in the different areas of the portrait using a variety of lines. Look at the key artwork and show how the artist has used directional lines to show the contours of the face and body. Also, highlight how the lines vary in length and width.

Plenary
Gather the children to look at their portraits and show good examples of use of line. Explain to the children that they will be transferring their designs onto tiles next lesson and demonstrate how to engrave the design onto the tile, tell them that they need to be gentle but firm to avoid making a hole in the tile.

Lesson 2 Making a printing tile

Key artwork
Elizabeth Catlett, *Sharecropper*, linoleum cut, 1952

You will need
- Children's drawings from last lesson
- Paper
- Pencils
- Erasers
- Foam tiles

Preparation

Prepare your own example tile, with a portrait incised into it.

Getting started

Look at the key artwork and remind the children that the white areas are the bits that were cut away or incised. Use you tile to demonstrate how the design will look once it is on the tile.

Class activities

- Give the children their tiles and ask them to transfer their design from paper onto the tile, asking them to press down hard but not so hard as to make a hole.

Plenary

Gather the children to look at their tiles and ensure that they have pressed hard enough so that they have an effect when printing next lesson.

Lesson 3 Printing

Key artwork

Elizabeth Catlett, *Sharecropper*, linoleum cut, 1952

You will need

- Printing ink
- Rollers for printing
- Tray palettes
- Paper
- Pencils
- Foam tiles with the children's designs on them
- Aprons

Preparation

Set the classroom up for printing, with the rollers and palettes accessible to all of the children, one between two works well.

Getting started

Demonstrate to the children how to print using their tile. Roll the ink out onto the tray palette and wait for the ink to make a sticky sound before applying it to the print tile. Then, place the paper over the tile and rub firmly all over. When the image feels like it has transferred, peel the paper away.

Class activities

- Remind the children to write their names on a few sheets of paper, in preparation for printing onto them.
- Allow the children to work in pairs or small groups to print a few copies of their work.

Further activities

1. The children could make a few prints and experiment with using watercolour paints to add colour to the dry print.

Cross-curricular links

History: Studies of Catlett could work well alongside studies of the Civil Rights Movement and slavery.

25 Sarah Eisenlohr: Human impact collage

In 30 seconds...

In these lessons, the children will learn about the work and techniques of Sarah Eisenlohr and how she uses collage as a medium to explore everyday issues and concepts to do with how human beings impact the planet they inhabit. The children will create their own collages inspired by the key artworks by exploring themes to do with humans and their environment.

Key artworks

Sarah Eisenlohr, *Preserve*, collage, 2012
Sarah Eisenlohr, *Settlers*, collage, 2012 (see Figure 25A)

What do I need to know?

Sarah Eisenlohr (born 1988) is a Montana-based graphic designer and artist. Her style is contemporary and reflects current trends in art, illustration and graphic design in addition to having a distinctively personal and original aesthetic. Prints of her collage work are available to purchase in a variety of formats at online shops, and her work has featured in many popular blogs and publications such as *Urban Outfitters* and *Vogue*. She has work in the permanent collection at Montana Museum of Art and Culture.

Eisenlohr became interested in collage after taking a course at college in which she was encouraged to combine maps and art media. She focused on producing a series of work around how humans 'remap' the landscape, and her love of collage grew from there. She uses vintage magazines, which can be challenging to source in Montana, a craft knife and paste to create her collages. Before digital manipulation was available to improve and embellish images, knives like the ones this artist cuts with were used for their precision, to literally cut and paste parts of images ready for print. Eisenlohr derives much joy out of using collage as a method and using her hands rather than a computer to manipulate images, seeing it as an important and refreshing break from screens, especially significant in the increasingly digital age we live in. As she also works as a graphic designer for a diverse range of clients, Sarah incorporates collage for design projects by scanning her handmade collage work then using photo editing software to create the finished graphic image.

Eisenlohr is greatly influenced by her surroundings and credits Montana's mountainous and nature-filled landscape as being inspirational for her work. Her collages often make reference to how humans derive enjoyment from nature and have the potential to change their surroundings by the way they interact with them, not always for the better. Her work sometimes invites the viewer to see planet Earth in the wider context of the universe – she uses subtle suggestion such as images that evoke the solar system or compositions that make us wonder what is beyond our planet. Eisenlohr often plays with proportions, contrasting images of people and landscapes by scaling them up or down to create a feeling of other-worldliness even though we are looking at familiar things. The collages suggest a narrative and often have an element of humour to them.

The key artworks are both from the artist's *Mapping* series, and Eisenlohr has transformed existing images of landscapes and architecture, from magazines, and showed the influence of people living and interacting with these places. In *Settlers*, the women are cultivating land on another planet because Earth, having been fully 'developed' is too full. In *Preserve*, a lady akin to a milkmaid is topping up the mountains with fake snow, as global warming has left the peaks of the mountains without any.

- Sarah Eisenlohr is a Montana-based **collage** artist and **graphic designer**.
- Before images could be **digitally manipulated**, craft knives were used to literally cut and paste images.
- The craft knife allows for **precision** cutting.
- Eisenlohr makes collages that invite the viewer to consider how human beings influence the landscape and whether we are transforming the planet for the better.
- Eisenlohr makes images that inspire questions about the dangers of **permanent** change to the **global environment**.
- Sarah's images often have a dream-like quality to them as she contrasts the **scale** of images to create compositions that are at once familiar and unfamiliar.
- The collages often suggest a **narrative**, the details of which are left to the viewer to compile.

Vocabulary

Collage: Art made by cutting and sticking various materials.
Digitally manipulated: An image that has been altered using image editing software.
Global environment: The environment of Earth in general.
Graphic designer: Someone who combines images and/or text to convey information to an audience with a specific effect.
Narrative: A story.
Permanent: Remaining changed forever.
Scale: The size of something.

Useful links

www.saraheisart.tumblr.com/post/27390913681/settlers Settlers
www.society6.com/saraheisenlohr Examples of the artist's work

Lesson 1 Humans and their environment

Key artworks
Sarah Eisenlohr, *Preserve*, collage, 2012
Sarah Eisenlohr, *Settlers*, collage, 2012

You will need
- A3 paper
- Pencils
- Erasers

Preparation
It may be useful to collect some images of examples of how humans impact the environment; these could be used to prompt the children when they come to the mind mapping task.

Getting started
Look at the key artworks with the children and ask them
to talk about what they see, describing the characters and what they are doing as well as the settings. Ask the children if they know how the artist made these images and explain they are collages made from old magazines. Explain what the common themes are in these images and discuss with the children their concerns about the planet and how human beings impact their own environments, sometimes detrimentally. You could show the children the images that you have collected to help them generate ideas.

Class activities
- Ask the children to work in pairs or groups to create a mind map of the different ways that human beings impact the Earth. If necessary, prompt the children with questions about how we pollute land, air and water and the impact of deforestation, urbanisation and global warming.
- Ask the children to share their ideas and note down any ideas from others' that they might want to use as collage inspiration. These should be issues that they feel strongly about.

Plenary
Gather the children to discuss their mind maps, asking them to share whether there are any issues that they feel particularly strongly about and why. Look at other examples of the artist's work (www.sarah-eisenlohr.com) and discuss how Sarah Eisenlohr places images together to create a composition that is not necessarily realistic but tells a story about how humans interact with the earth. Note how the collage is carefully put together so that the image looks like one seamless picture.

Lesson 2 A narrative composition

Key artworks
Sarah Eisenlohr, *Preserve*, collage, 2012
Sarah Eisenlohr, *Settlers*, collage, 2012

You will need
- Magazines
- A3 paper containing mind maps from previous lesson
- A3 or A4 paper for sticking onto, one each
- Glue sticks or PVA with spreaders
- Envelopes or folders to store loose images in
- Scissors

Preparation
Collect a selection of magazines and newspapers for children to cut images from; you might need to supplement these with printed pictures that are relevant, e.g. pictures of planet Earth, factories emitting pollution, etc. The children will be using these to collage their final compositions from. Place the images in piles that are easily accessible to the children, so they can search through and find suitable sections for their work.

Getting started
Look at the key artworks with the children and remind the children about the way that the artist has cut seamlessly so that the images do not appear to be cut and pasted together. Demonstrate to the children how to broadly cut around areas in order to then focus on cutting around smaller sections. Remind the children how the collages by Eisenlohr seem to be telling a story and ask them to explore different compositions before committing to sticking images together. Bring the children's attention to how the scale of images can vary and do not need to be realistic in order for the composition to work well. Tell the children that they will now work individually to sort through magazines, newspapers, etc. to find images to make their collage, and remind the children that their collage should tell a story about humans and how they treat planet earth.

Class activities
- Allow the children to look through magazines to find images that could be used for their collage – they will need to collect images for settings, characters and props.
- Ask the children to create a collage which shows human beings interacting, influencing or permanently changing the planet.
- The children should play with scale and ensure that their collages do not look obviously collaged – tell them that before digital manipulation was possible, manual cutting was the only option.
- Remind the children to consult their mind maps from the previous lesson to help them with ideas.
- The children can store any loose cuttings in the envelopes, ready for next lesson.

Plenary
Gather the children to discuss their work so far, asking the children to comment on each other's work and 'read' the narrative in the collages.

Lesson 3 A series of collages

Key artworks
Sarah Eisenlohr, *Preserve*, collage, 2012
Sarah Eisenlohr, *Settlers*, collage, 2012

You will need
- Magazines
- A3 paper containing mind maps from previous lesson
- Children's collage work from the previous lesson
- A3 or A4 paper for sticking onto
- Glue sticks or PVA with spreaders
- Envelopes or folders to store loose images in
- Scissors
- A thesaurus

Preparation
Set out the materials gathered for the previous lesson again, along with any new magazines or newspapers you've been able to find. Ensure that the material is easily accessible to the children, so they can search through and find suitable sections for their work.

Getting started
Begin by looking at the key artworks and bring the children's attention to the titles of the works and how they add a dimension of understanding to the concepts in the work. Explain that the children will need to think of one word titles for each of their collages and that the titles should summarise the concept being depicted in their work. Explain that artists sometimes create a series of work about the same theme and tell them that today they can create more collages to go with their theme.

Class activities
- Ask the children to use their mind maps to create another collage.
- Ask the children to create a title for each piece and write a paragraph about the concepts in their collage. They can use a thesaurus to help with this.

Plenary
Gather the children to discuss their work, asking the children to comment on each other's work and 'read' the narrative in the collages. Ask the children to present their favourite piece, explaining why and talking about the concept in relation to the global environment.

Further activities

1. The children could develop their most successful collage into a piece of graphic design, by scanning the image and using image editing software. You could set them a brief as if they have been employed by a company or organisation to raise awareness of environmental issues through a poster.

Cross-curricular links

Geography: These collages would work well alongside a topic about humans and their environment, and climate change.

Glossary

Aborigines: The indigenous people of Australia.

Advertising: Calling the public's attention to a product or service, e.g. via television, newspapers, magazines, radio, the Internet, billboards, posters, endorsements, etc.

Amate: Bark paper used by Mayans and Aztecs.

Andamento: The visual flow of a mosaic.

Architect: A person who designs buildings and often supervises the construction.

Artist: A person who creates art.

Artistic style: A distinctive way of working, which can permit grouping of works.

Arts and Crafts Movement: A movement in the decorative and fine arts that began in Britain and spread to Europe and North America between 1880 and 1910.

Balanced composition: The arrangement of the formal elements of art in relation to each other.

Billboard: A large outdoor board for displaying advertisements – billboard designs are more frequently made using graphic reproduction now, but historically they were hand-painted.

Box easel: A freestanding easel that includes a compartment to store paints and brushes, etc. – some also include a handle or straps so they can be carried like a backpack or suitcase.

Brushstroke: The mark made by a paintbrush.

Classical: Of an exemplary standard within a traditional and long-established style.

Collage: Art made by cutting and sticking various materials.

Collography (also spelled collagraphy): A printmaking process.

Colourful: Having lots of varied bright colour.

Commission: To order the production of something.

Composition: Combining parts to make a whole.

Concept: An idea.

Conceptual: Based on ideas.

Construct: To build something.

Contemporary art: Art that is produced in the present day or in the recent past.

Controversial: Causing disagreement and dividing opinion.

Conventional: In accordance with what is generally done.

Craftspeople: People skilled at making things.

Cross-hatching: Shading with lines that cross over.

Cubist: A style whereby diverse views of the subject (usually objects or figures) come together in the same picture, resulting in images that appear fragmented and abstracted. Invented in around 1907/08 by artists Pablo Picasso and Georges Braque.

Decorative: Something made to look attractive.

Decorative arts: Art and crafts produced for both aesthetic value and functionality.

Design: A plan or drawing made to depict the look and function or workings of a building, garment, or another object before it is made.

Detail: Small features that could be difficult to notice.

Digitally manipulated: An image that has been altered using image editing software.

Direct observation: Collecting information by watching the subject at first hand.

Dot painting: Painting made using dots rather than brush strokes

Draughtsman: A person skilled in drawing.

Draw: To produce a picture or diagram using lines and marks.

En plein air: A French phrase meaning 'open (in full) air', and refers to the way that. Impressionist artists painted outdoors.

Engrave: To cut a design on a surface.

Enlarge: To make something larger.

Exhibition: A public display of work or art.

Figurative art: Any form of art that retains strong references to the real world, and particularly to the human figure.

Geometric forms: three-dimensional shapes such as cylinders and pyramids.

Geometric shapes: Made of regular lines, shapes such as squares, triangles, or rectangles.

Goldsmith: A person who makes items out of gold.

High art: A concept used by societies to describe art that is created by a culturally-renowned and accepted artist.

Graphic designer: Someone who combines images and/or text to convey information to an audience with a specific effect.

Handmade crafts: Made by hand, not by machine.

Homage: Something done with respect to, or acknowledgement of another or another's work.

Hue: A colour.

Indigenous: Originating from a place.

Individualistic: Being characteristic of that person.

Imagination: Using the mind to create new ideas.

Impression: An idea, feeling or opinion about something or someone, often formed on first contact.

Impressionism: A style of painting developed in the last third of the nineteenth century.

Juxtapose: To place subjects together or close by for contrast or comparison.

Landmark: A feature of a landscape or town that is easily seen and recognised.

Line: A long mark or stroke.

Linoleum cut: A printmaking technique, a variant of woodcut, in which a sheet of linoleum is cut into.

Manipulate: Control in a skilful manner.

Manufactured: To make something using machinery.

Maquette: A small preliminary model or sketch.

Mass-produced: The production or manufacture of goods in large quantities.

Materials: Things from which other things can be made.

Memory: Something remembered from the past.

Meticulously: Showing extreme care and being precise.

Mineral: A naturally occurring material.

Mood: A state of mind or feeling.

Mosaic: A piece of art made by assembling small pieces of glass, ceramics or other materials.

Mural: A large painting made on or fixed to a wall.

Narrative: A story.

Natural pigment: An organically found substance that gives something a colour when it is added to it, such as in plants, flowers and fruits.

Non-traditional: Not according to the usual traditions.

Opulence: Lavishness or wealth.

Opus regulatum: A design where the tesserae form a regular grid pattern.

Opus palladianum: A design where the tesserae vary in size and shape and are placed haphazardly

Organic forms: In art, shapes that are often flowing and unpredictable in contrast to geometric shapes.

Origami: Japanese art of paper folding; the word is derived from two Japanese words: 'ori' meaning to fold and 'kami' meaning paper.

Original print: A print that is made directly from the artists' own woodblock or printing plate and printed by the artist.

Origins: Where something begins, or is derived; its birthplace.

Ornamental: Intended as decoration.

Painter: A person who paints as a profession or is very talented at it.

Papyrus: An ancient Egyptian paper made from the pith of a river plant.

Patron: A person who gives support to an individual or organisation.

Pattern: A repeated design.

Pendant: A piece of jewellery that hangs from a chain around the neck.

Pop art: An art movement that was extremely popular in the 1960s in America and Britain. Pop artists get inspiration from popular and commercial culture such as advertising. Other pop artists include Andy Warhol, Claes Oldenburg, Roy Lichtenstein, Peter Blake and David Hockney.

Popular culture: Activities, interests or products suited to the mainstream tastes of the masses.

Prehistoric: A time before recorded history.

Preparatory: Done to get ready for something.

Primary colours: A group of colours that cannot be created using other colours.

Print: A mark made on a surface.

Printing press: A machine for printing text or pictures from plates or woodblocks.

Printmaker: An artist who makes pictures or designs by printing them from plates or blocks.

Production: The process of making something from raw materials.

Proportion: A part, share, or number considered in comparative relation to a whole.

Regional: Relating to a particular area.

Relief: A type of sculpture in which the work projects *from* but is attached to a wall, or other type of background surface, on which it is carved.

Represent: To stand for or symbolise.

Revolutionised: To change something radically.

Salon: In nineteenth century France, the Salon was the official annual art exhibition in France; it was where all the esteemed artists would exhibit their work, and where important figures in French society would gather to discuss art and culture.

Scale: The size of something.

Sculptor: An artist who makes sculptures.

Sculpture: A three-dimensional representative or abstract form.

Secondary colours: Colours resulting from the mixing of two of the primary colours.

Self-taught: Gaining knowledge and skill on your own, rather than through taught education.

Semi-abstract: The subject remains recognisable although the forms may be stylised.

Shade: A darker version of an original colour made by adding black.

Shape: The form or outline of an object.

Simplify: To make something easier to understand.

Still life: A genre of art typically depicting inanimate objects on a surface.

Symbolise: Represent or stand for something.

Symbols: Something used to represent something else.

Tempera: A quick-drying paint made by mixing coloured pigments with egg and sometimes oil or water.

Tesserae: Small pieces of a material used to make a mosaic.

Texture: The feel or perceived feel of a surface.

Three-dimensional: Not flat (two-dimensional) and therefore appearing real.

Tint: A lighter version of an original colour made by adding white.

Tone: The lightness or darkness of something.

Turner Prize: An art award given every year to a British artist under 50 years of age.

Unconventional: Not the usual.

Visual texture: A representation of texture that an artist creates using line, tone and colour.

Woodblock print: A technique for printing text, images or patterns used extensively throughout East Asia and originating in China.

Bibliography

Da Vinci, L. (2010), *The Writings of Leonardo Da Vinci*. California: Golgotha Press.

DfE (2013), *National curriculum in England: Art and design programmes of study: key stages 1 and 2*. London: Crown.

Morris, W. (1894), *The Wood Beyond the World*. London: Kelmscott Press

Petherbridge, D. (2010), *The Primacy of Drawing: Histories and Theories of Practice*. (First edition) London: Yale University Press.

Reader, M. (2009), *Seven wasted men*. [online] Available at: www.michelle-reader.co.uk/archive/seven-wasted-men.html

Robinson, K. (2006) *Ken Robinson: Do schools kill creativity?* [Video file] Available at: www.ted.com/talks/ken_robinson_says_schools_kill_creativity

Rosenquist, J. & Dalton, D. (2010) *Painting Below Zero*. New York: Alfred A. Knopf

Solomon, D. (2005), *Pretty in Paint*. [online] Available at: www.nytimes.com/2005/02/27/magazine/pretty-in-paint.html?_r=0

O'Keeffe, G. (1939) *Flowers and still life*. Available at: www.tate.org.uk/whats-on/tate-modern/exhibition/georgia-okeeffe/room-guide/room-six

Van Gogh, V. (1998), *The Letters of Vincent van Gogh*. (3rd printing edition) London: Penguin

Useful links

Art history

30 must-see paintings and the National Gallery London with information about each painting: www.nationalgallery.org.uk/paintings/explore-the-paintings/30-highlight-paintings
Extensive art history information in chronological order: www.metmuseum.org/toahchronology
Online learning forum covering many subjects including art history: www.khanacademy.org/humanities/art-history
Overview of historical periods and art genres: www.arthistory.net

General art

Games and videos for children: kids.tate.org.uk
Glossary of art terms: www.tate.org.uk/learn/online-resources/glossary
The National Curriculum: www.gov.uk/government/uploads/system/uploads/attachment_data/file/239018/PRIMARY_national_curriculum_-_Art_and_design.pdf
Resource for zooming into a selection of artworks: www.google.com/culturalinstitute/about/artproject

Techniques

Video tutorials on different media and techniques: www.bbc.co.uk/schools/gcsebitesize/art/practicalities/mediaandtechniques1.shtml

Acknowledgements

Quotations from National Curriculum documents used in this publication are approved under an Open Government Licence: www.nationalarchives.gov.uk/doc/open-government-licence/version/3/

Image credits

Figure 1A © DEA PICTURE LIBRARY/Getty Images
Figure 1B © Ralph Morse/Getty Images
Figure 3A © Heritage Images/Getty Images
Figure 4A © Andy Goldsworthy
Figure 5A © Kiev.Victor/Shutterstock.com
Figure 7A © Photo 12/Getty Images
Figure 11A © Historical Picture Archive/Getty Images
Figure 12A © Richard Sweeney
Figure 21A © Print Collector/Getty Images
Figure 25A © Sarah Eisenlohr
Figure 1C, 1D, 3B, 3C, 7B, 7C, 11B, 11C, 12B, 12C, 21B and 21C © Emily Gopaul